UNDUE PROCESS

THE FREE PRESS
A Division of Macmillan, Inc.
NEW YORK

Maxwell Macmillan Canada
TORONTO

Maxwell Macmillan International
NEW YORK   OXFORD   SINGAPORE   SYDNEY

ELLIOTT ABRAMS

UNDUE PROCESS

*A Story of How
Political Differences
Are Turned Into Crimes*

The Free Press
A Division of Macmillan, Inc.
866 Third Avenue, New York, N.Y. 10022

Maxwell Macmillan Canada, Inc.
1200 Eglinton Avenue East
Suite 200
Don Mills, Ontario M3C 3N1

Macmillan, Inc. is part of the Maxwell Communication
Group of Companies.

Printed in the United States of America

printing number
1 2 3 4 5 6 7 8 9 10

Library of Congress Cataloging-in-Publication Data

Abrams, Elliott
    Undue process: a story of how political differences are turned
into crimes / Elliott Abrams.
        p.   cm.
    Includes index.
    ISBN 0–02–900167–6
    1. Iran-Contra Affair, 1985–1990. 2. Abrams, Elliott.
I. Title.
E876.A28   1993
955.05—dc20   92–24945
                                                  CIP

To my mother
MILDRED ABRAMS
and to the memory of my father
JOSEPH ABRAMS

CONTENTS

CONTENTS

Judgments   209

Afterword   231

Index   235

PREFACE

W hen I emerged from eight years at the State Department in 1989, everyone I knew—or so it seemed—advised me to write a memoir about the experience. That was not the book I wanted to write, for I had no desire to dwell on the events of the mid-1980s or on U.S. policy in Central America. Instead, I had in mind a broader look at the history, and the future, of American foreign policy. The Hudson Institute named me a Senior Fellow, and I began happily to write that foreign policy book in 1990.

I had to put it aside in the summer of 1991, when my life was disrupted, then wrenched off its course, by the "Office of Independent Counsel," which is charged with investigating and prosecuting what is now known as the Iran/Contra scandal. As the prosecutors began to focus on me, I began to keep a journal of what was happening. From that journal, and from memory, I have tried to reconstruct here the story of my prosecution, plea bargain, and sentencing.

This book was begun with a grant from the Historical Research Foundation and was written with the generous support of the Lynde and Harry Bradley Foundation, both of which I am very happy to acknowledge. I am most grateful to Midge Decter for editing the manuscript, and to Erwin Glikes for his encouragement, advice, and help. My wife, Rachel, was as always my first reader and my best critic. This book would not have been written at all without her enthusiastic and constant support, and it benefited immeasurably from her talents.

I have tried to portray an experience very few Americans will ever have—and none ever should. Congress should not be permitted to suspend our system of justice and to force the selection of special prosecutors whose job it is to target individuals and try—at any expense—to pin crimes on them. Political differences should not be turned into crimes.

This kind of prosecution is something new in America, and it is wrong. My own prosecution was not the first, but I hope it will be one of the last. That is why I decided to tell this story.

INTRODUCTION

Law, Politics, and Scandal

O n October 7, 1991, I pleaded guilty in the U.S. District Court for the District of Columbia to two counts of withholding information from Congress, a crime under Section 192 of Title Two of the United States Code. On November 15, 1991, the Court placed me on two years' probation, with one hundred hours of community service as a condition of probation, and suspended imposition of a sentence.

One year earlier—or sixteen years earlier, when I first arrived in Washington—I could not even have contemplated a criminal conviction. I would have considered it ludicrous, impossible, insane.

I came to Washington in March 1975 as a young lawyer, less than two years out of law school and bored with corporate legal work. During the 1972 presidential primaries I had gotten to know Senator Henry M. "Scoop" Jackson, the Democrat from Washington State, who was testing out a presidential run and wanted to be on the ballot in Massachusetts. Scoop Jackson was a hard-liner on foreign policy issues and was beginning to attract the support of many Democrats who, like me, felt the Truman–Kennedy–Johnson foreign policy line

1

of activist anti-Communism should be extended. I believed a strong and vigorous America was truly the last, best hope of freedom in the world.

In 1972, in my second year at Harvard Law School, I, along with a few other Harvard students, had done volunteer work for Scoop, going door to door in Boston to get his ballot petitions signed. I had taken time away from classes to work for him in the Florida primary as well, and had told Jackson that if he ran for President in 1976, I'd like to be on his staff.

By January 1975, Wall Street law no longer intrigued me. I used my spare time writing magazine articles and book reviews on politics and foreign policy, and I had come to the conclusion that I didn't want to work on foreign affairs part-time. I wanted to put all my energy into it, and I asked Scoop for a job. He said "Come on down," so I found an apartment and joined his Senate staff. I knew Scoop's chances were slim in the 1976 elections, and I planned to return to New York after November. Like so many other young lawyers, however, I loved Washington and I loved politics, and I wanted to stay. Daniel P. Moynihan was elected Senator from New York that November, and I had worked with him during the Jackson campaign. When he offered me a job as his Special Counsel, acting really as chief legislative assistant, I jumped at it.

I stayed with Moynihan for two and a half years, ending up as his chief of staff, and then decided to try law practice again in the hope that "Washington law" would be different and more fun. After a year of it I wanted to go back to working in the government.

By this time, I had given up on the Democrats; after nominating McGovern and Carter, the party seemed to me clearly now wedded to a foreign policy I could not accept. Everyone in my family was a Democrat, and the decision to support the Republicans did not come easily, but the Democratic Party no longer represented my strongly held views. Indeed it flatly rejected them, and many of us who had backed Senator Jackson in 1976 found ourselves switching parties in 1980. I hoped Reagan, with his spirited anti-Communism and his call for American military strength, would win, and I volunteered to work on his campaign. I spent much of September and October of 1980 in campaign work, and when Reagan did win, I looked for a position on the transition team and in the new Administration.

Foreign policy was my true love, and it was what had led me to support Reagan, so it was what I wanted to work on. When a campaign acquaintance offered me a position on the Agency for International Development transition team, I accepted with alacrity. It was as fascinating, and as much fun, as I had hoped; I went to work each day in the State Department building overflowing with enthusiasm. This was what I wanted to do for the next few years, I was certain, and I set my sights on a position in the State Department. I knew that at thirty-two I was too young for a very important position. Calculating that everyone associated my former boss, Pat Moynihan, with the United Nations (where he had made such a splash as U.S. Ambassador in the late 1970s), I decided that the powers that be might find me most qualified for one of the Deputy Assistant Secretary of State posts in the bureau that handles the U.N., the International Organizations Bureau. When I told Moynihan what I hoped to ask the Reagan personnel office for, he raised an eyebrow: Why *Deputy* Assistant Secretary, he asked? Ask for Assistant Secretary! What the hell! I did, and after a good round of pushing and shoving among the personnel people, got it.

The job had many satisfactions, not least the full Assistant Secretary rank. But there were two problems. First, real influence over U.S. policy toward the U.N. rested with the U.S. Ambassador, Jeane Kirkpatrick, and in the time-honored and probably inescapable turf fighting between the State Department and her office in New York I was caught in the middle. Second, the work left to me involved the U.N.'s European agencies—the International Labor Organization, World Health Organization, and the like—and though it was important, it was peripheral to the issues that had brought me into government.

In the summer of 1981, I was asked to help the Administration think through what might be done with the State Department's Bureau of Human Rights and Humanitarian Affairs. Reaganites saw it as a relic of the Carter foreign policy, and the new Administration's candidate to take charge of it had had to withdraw his name after running into a Senate buzz saw. It was now a bureaucratic wreck, for months without leadership, its staff leaving and its mission confused. Compared with the International Organizations Bureau, it was smaller, less prestigious, and less influential. But as I thought about it, I wanted the job. Human rights! This was what American foreign policy should be all about; this was what separated us from the Communist world. Here was a chance for me to make a real contribution, explaining to the Left that any serious human rights policy had to be strongly anti-Communist, and to the Right that fighting right-wing—as well as Communist—dictatorships must be a matter of principle for the United States. This was the kind of thing I had come to Washington for. Developing a Reaganite human rights policy was a dream assignment for me.

I asked for the job and, in December 1981, got it. For three and a half years I tried to rebuild the bureau and expound a conservative theory of human rights. When in the summer of 1982 George Shultz became Secretary of State, the job became easier and more fun, because he cared deeply about human rights issues. I had easy access to him, he liked the work we were doing, and in the internecine warfare that characterizes the State Department he gave my bureau enough victories to make us a bureaucratic "player" for the first time. Other bureaus in the Department sometimes accused us of elevating human rights over national security matters, while many Democrats in Congress accused us of the opposite, of burying human rights concerns under other Administration foreign policy goals. For me and my staff, both career diplomats and political appointees, this intellectual and political combat went with the territory. I embraced it, enjoyed it, and encouraged it.

In the spring of 1985 I received a telephone call from Shultz's chief assistant. The Assistant Secretary for Inter-American Affairs was leaving. Would I take the job if the Secretary offered it to me? If the answer was yes, he wanted to see me that afternoon. The answer was yes.

This would not be going from the frying pan into the fire, I knew; I would be going from the pantry into a bonfire burning with very high flames. Even in ordinary times, running one of the Department's "geographical" bureaus was a hugely bigger job than running the Human Rights Bureau. My staff would grow from twenty-five to two hundred;

UNDUE PROCESS

I would be responsible for the three dozen U.S. embassies in Latin America and the Caribbean; I would deal with Latin presidents, with the Defense Department and the CIA, and with the White House and the National Security Council (NSC), regularly. I would not write about policy, I would help formulate it and implement it.

But those were not ordinary times. There was a war on, or rather there were two: a guerrilla war in Central America, and an almost equally violent political war about Central America between the Reagan Administration and the Democratic-controlled Congress. Two men had already held the job of Assistant Secretary of State for Inter-American Affairs under President Reagan, each one burned up by those political flames in a couple of years. I knew that if I approached this new position as I had the Human Rights job, embracing the need to do battle for the President's policies, there would be plenty of sparks. Yet I could see no other way to do the job well: the President and his policies were under fierce attack, and a fierce defense was called for. I believed deeply in the policy of defending democracy in Latin America, and that meant not only opposing military dictators of the Right, but hitting hard at the Leftist forces being armed and encouraged by the Soviet Union and Cuba. I approached the fight with enthusiasm, undeterred by friends' warnings of the political dangers ahead.

President Reagan had come into office after a decade of American setbacks: the loss in Vietnam, the Marxist victory in Angola, the fall of the Shah of Iran, the Soviet invasion of Afghanistan, the Marxist coup in Grenada, and then Nicaragua. In July 1979, the Somoza dictatorship in Nicaragua had been overthrown. The new government had been quickly taken over by a Marxist-Leninist group called the Sandinistas, and they had proceeded to establish close ties with Castro's Cuba and with the Soviet Union. There was persuasive evidence of Sandinista subversion of neighboring countries, especially El Salvador, and by the time President Carter had left office he had suspended U.S. aid to Nicaragua because of that subversion.

As part of his policy of ending Soviet expansionism and reasserting American power, Reagan wanted Central America pacified and the Sandinistas out. He increased U.S. military aid to El Salvador, Honduras, and Guatemala, and ordered the CIA to support an armed rebellion against Sandinista rule. The CIA program of support for the Nicaraguan Resistance, the "Contras," began in late 1981, but Democratic opposition was fierce. If Reagan saw Nicaragua as a key test of American resolve because it was the only U.S.-Soviet battleground on the American mainland, much of the Democratic leadership saw it as yet another immoral episode of Yankee imperialism in the Americas.

Congress began restricting the Contra program in 1982, with the first "Boland Amendment." This prohibited spending aimed at "overthrowing" the Sandinista government (as opposed to interfering with its subversion of its neighbors). In October 1984 another Boland Amendment cut off Contra aid entirely, prohibiting any agency involved in intelligence activities from any spending to assist military operations against the Government of Nicaragua directly or indirectly. Later variants of the Boland Amendment—it is important to know that there were five altogether, all of them appropriations measures, none a criminal statute, and each more opaque than the last—permitted intelligence sharing with the Contras and humanitarian aid to them. Finally, on October 17, 1986, Congress reversed direction and approved $100 million in military as well as humanitarian support for the Contras.

I was sworn in as Assistant Secretary of State for Inter-American Affairs on July 17, 1985. Shortly thereafter, on August 15, Congress voted $27 million in humanitarian assistance for the Contras, and the State Department was largely in charge of managing it. I and my associates in the Administration spent the next year trying to battle the Sandinistas with one arm and fight off the Democrats in Congress with the other. During the time the U.S. Government was supplying the Contras with humanitarian aid—boots, uniforms, medicines—a network of private citizens sprang up to supply them with guns and ammunition. I and my staff, and everyone else handling Central America, walked a tightrope, wishing to encourage that private network but aware that we were prohibited by law from involvement with it.

I had held the job for sixteen months when the "Iran/Contra Affair" broke, and it was announced that profits from secret arms sales to Iran had been diverted to the Contras. A huge political scandal ensued, rocking the Administration and leading to three investigations: joint hearings held by special committees of the House and Senate, a commission headed by the late Senator John Tower at the behest of the President, and a criminal investigation conducted by a special prosecutor. I testified in each, and—despite a clamor from many Democrats for my resignation—held onto my job because of strong support from Secretary Shultz. I left office when the Reagan Administration ended, on January 20, 1989.

What follows is an account of what happened to me some five years after that scandal erupted, at first to my disbelief, and at last to my anger that these events could take place in this country.

JOURNAL, 1991

Walsh Breaks His Silence

I had last heard from the Office of Independent Counsel, the "OIC," headed by a retired federal judge named Lawrence Walsh, more than two years before. In June 1987, following the Congressional Iran/Contra hearings, I had appeared three times before the grand jury convened to investigate the affair. By then it was clear that Oliver North had coordinated the activities of the private network helping the Contras, and the central question addressed to me was whether I had known this in 1985 and 1986. In fact, I and my colleagues had believed North was the Administration's liaison with this private network, but not in charge of it. I had assured Secretary Shultz, the Congress, and the press that the U.S. Government was not running this network. It was now clear that I had been wrong; Walsh's question was whether I had been lying. The answer was no.

Then, in early 1988, Walsh's assistant, Geoffrey Stewart, had informed my lawyer, W. DeVier Pierson, that they believed what I was saying and that they appreciated my cooperation. I had been interviewed by Stewart and his assistant, Jeffrey Toobin, several times and had appeared before the grand jury, as I said, three times, and now it was over.

In the following three years, I heard from Walsh's office directly not one single time, and indirectly only once: in early 1991, young Mr. Toobin published a book titled *Opening Arguments,* which was his account of his part in the investigation. In it, he made plain a startling bias on the part of the OIC staff. Toobin himself had jumped at the chance to work on my case, he related; he had sought it out, and though we had never met, his motivation was quite clear: personal animus and political hatred. Others on the staff, he revealed, shared the same outlook, so my own early speculation about the nature of the staff Walsh had assembled proved accurate. Its members were primarily liberal and Democratic, and motivated by a nasty mix of personal ambition, ideology, and animus. They were after scalps and had only very reluctantly concluded they could not get mine.

Indeed, while Stewart had told my lawyer they had concluded I was telling the truth, in Toobin's book he was quoted as asserting that I was a liar and a criminal, but that the evidence against me was not strong enough to permit bringing a case. Did Stewart lie to my lawyer? Or did Toobin lie about Stewart?

Whatever the answer, I actually felt that *Opening Arguments,* revealing as it did on the one hand the absolute bias of the prosecutors against me, and on the other their inability to find any evidence against me, was a small protection. Surely, after this they would have to drop the investigation.

But at the same time, in early 1991, friends and former colleagues were beginning to tell me that they had been questioned about me by Walsh's staff. Not all the questions were about me, these people reported, but most were. Some were brought before the grand jury to answer such questions. And I was certain that if these friends had called me, surely there were others too scared to tell me about their questioning, and still others, not friends at all, questioned as well. Something was up.

Moreover, I was convinced Walsh's office had been persistently leaking information to newspapers. Throughout the winter and spring articles appeared announcing that the investigation of me was continuing, or that the focus was again turning to me. Walsh's staff seemed to be able to leak with impunity. There was never a complaint against them. Leaks against conservatives did not reverberate, it seemed, and no reporter or congressional committee showed the slightest interest in pursuing the Independent Counsel's office on this account. Only stories based on leaks against leading Democrats had repercussions. In May 1989, for example, someone in the Justice Department or the FBI had told reporters that there was an investigation being conducted of Congressman Bill Gray, then the House Democratic Whip. When the stories began to appear, a year-long scandal erupted that included accusations and recriminations about the horrors of prosecutorial leaking. In relation to me, not a sound was heard.

It seemed that Walsh and his boys were still pursuing me, and that they had in mind a prosecution based on the allegation that some statements of mine—out of the million and one I had made to Congress—were not accurate. They had, my lawyer theorized, apparently abandoned their efforts to find governmentwide violations of the Boland Amendment, or conspiracies to violate it, and were now operating on a new theory, one that would be easier to prove: that someone who had appeared before Congress on a score of occasions had at one time testified one way, at another time added more information, and at yet another time said much less. Or that someone who perhaps possessed certain information had in one or another piece of testimony not imparted it all. This legal theory, all things considered, would lead them to pursue me.

In the summer of 1991, they got a guilty plea from Alan Fiers, who had headed the CIA's Central America Task Force, and indicted Clair George, who had been the Agency's Deputy Director for Operations, under this theory. The two of them had sat side by side with me at several hearings, and I understood the implications of this new development, particularly Alan Fiers's plea, for me. I had had very few contacts with Clair George. As a Deputy Director of the CIA, he had operated at a higher level than mine in the Administration. Though I had the highest regard for him, we had never worked together, and I believed that whatever his problems with Walsh, they would be unlikely to affect me.

With Alan Fiers it was different. During those sixteen months between my accepting the Inter-American Affairs job and the breaking of Iran/Contra—July 1985 to November 1986—we had been in touch nearly every day, seen each other several times a week, shared many secrets, been friends and close allies, and had as well, against this background of collegiality, often fought each other like dogs.

Except for our commitment to the cause and our willingness to work very long hours, month after month, year after year, Fiers and I were nothing alike. He was from Ohio, had played football for Woody Hayes, and had pursued a career as an officer in the clandestine service after emerging from the military. I was a Harvard-trained neoconservative intellectual, a Jew from New York. When we met, shortly after my appointment to the Inter-American Affairs bureau, I was emerging from my post as Assistant Secretary of State for Human Rights, an office the CIA had never viewed as central to world affairs or to its own role in them.

Fiers had at once been my colleague and, I used to joke with my staff, my control officer, charged with making sure that I did not get in the way of Agency operations. Our responsibilities overlapped only in part: as chief of the CIA'a Central America Task Force, he was spending every minute of his time on the struggle in that region. For me, though it was the single most important commitment, there were many others as well—Mexico, Cuba, Haiti, Jamaica, Guyana, Argentina, Chile, and Paraguay, to name a few—and my exact counterpart at the Agency had been Fiers's superior, the Chief of the Latin America Division in the Directorate of Operations. Nevertheless, the emotional and intellectual bond, and struggle, had been between Alan and me. I had cooperated with him each day, as my staff had with his, to advance our policy, fight the battles with the Democratic majority in Congress, fight the Sandinistas, and cajole and reassure our Central American allies. For both of us, it was an honor to be fighting in one of the last battles of the Cold War. The Reagan Doctrine, ensuring the end of Soviet expansionism, had been put in the hands of a small group of officials, and we were proud and happy to be among them.

At the same time, our agencies had fought, and our teams had fought, for preeminence. Who would really influence the government of Guatemala or Honduras? Who would really influence the President of the United States? Who would really, in the most intense and longest-fought contest of all, control the Contras? We had stood shoulder to shoulder against common enemies, all the while struggling between ourselves for power.

I admired Fiers and his men greatly but believed that we at State were better suited in some ways for the job ahead. The CIA had not, my guys and I felt, fully grasped the ideological side of the struggle against the Sandinista regime. They knew which rifles the Contras needed, but when it came to doctrine, to political message and coloration, we were the ones with the savvy. The CIA had set up a Contra army all right, but that early army—called the FDN, the Spanish initials for "Nicaraguan Democratic Force"—had been exclusively a right-wing preserve, of precisely the sort Nicaraguans would never accept. The Sandinistas would never be beaten by ex-Somocistas; only a strategy that embraced "fulfilling the promise of the Revolution" could undermine their rule. Thus while the CIA had supported the FDN, we had tried to broaden the membership of the Contra command to include social democrats; while they had been averse to extremely independent actors like Eden Pastora, a former Sandinista commander then in self-imposed exile in Costa Rica, for us these had been the most credible leaders and therefore precisely the ones we wanted to recruit. While the Agency had usually viewed human rights abuses as an ugly but negligible accompaniment of war, we had seen them as an abomination that scarred the Contra effort and handed useful weapons to its opponents. We had fought endlessly over this issue. Agency people had considered us romantic and naïve, while we had been certain our political and ideological approach was the only road to victory.

But in the fall of 1991, the prosecutors did not want to hear about the struggles that had taken place between Fiers and me. They were convinced we had known the same secrets, and that we had sat side by side and told Congress otherwise.

It had earlier been a summer of joy and escape for my family and me. While our children were away at summer camp in July, my wife and I had spent ten days in California driving along the Coast Highway and visiting friends. Oh yes, my heart had skipped a beat for a moment when we read in the papers on July 9 about Alan Fiers's guilty plea. But the more I read the more I relaxed. Fiers's situation was entirely different from mine; he had, according to his statement, known of the arms sales to Iran and the diversion of money to the Contras early in the game, and had been ordered by a superior officer to leave it out of his testimony. I had learned of it, with everyone else, when the story broke. All things considered, it appeared he had been privy to a great deal of information that had never been shared with me. So while I read the news about him with great care, his case was not my case. I turned back to family matters. In August we went to the shore in Delaware for a family vacation, and it provided a wonderful illusion of escape.

But upon our return to Washington, Judge Walsh was waiting. He had pursued Alan Fiers until he had extracted from him a guilty plea and information that Walsh claimed incriminated Clair George. He and his staff were now persuaded that their methods and theory of the case had been vindicated. Now they might pursue me, secure in the belief that I could, and perhaps would, turn over a bigger fish, as Fiers had apparently done.

Throughout 1991 my lawyer, W. DeVier Pierson, and I had debated sending a letter to Walsh, mentioning the press stories and asking him to honor an old agreement with Geoffrey Stewart that they would never act against me in any way without first informing me. We had not sent the letter, reasoning under a fine old legal precept: let sleeping dogs lie. But as September 1991 came, and it was clear that those dogs were barking, the letter was dispatched. It was dated September 6, 1991, a Friday, and here is what it said:

Dear Judge Walsh:

I am writing to you on behalf of my client, Elliott Abrams.

As you know, Mr. Abrams has cooperated fully with you and your staff, including giving a number of interviews and providing testimony to the grand jury. During this time, Geoffrey Stewart of your staff repeatedly assured me that Mr. Abrams was not a target of the investigation and that I would be advised if there was any change in his status. With the exception of a call regarding a possible appearance by Mr. Abrams at proceedings before Judge Gesell in the North case, I have had no contact of any kind from your office for several years.

Since a number of recent news stories have mentioned Mr. Abrams in connection with your ongoing investigation, I felt it was appropriate to bring to your attention the understanding I have with your office. I assume that this understanding remains in effect so that I would be advised—and given the opportunity to meet with you—if there were to be any change in Mr. Abrams' status.

Kindest regards.

       Sincerely,

       W. DeVier Pierson

TUESDAY, SEPTEMBER 10

"And There Is Movement"

O n Tuesday, September 10, Walsh's new chief assistant, Craig Gillen, called Pierson to say that the letter had been handed to him by Judge Walsh and that he had been planning to call in any event. For there was indeed continued interest in my case. "And," he said, "there is movement."

"And there is movement." From the moment those words were uttered to me, time began moving at the speed of light, events crowding in each day, my sleep interrupted or delayed each night by endless internal arguments over what would happen and what to do about it, a kind of brain fever that brought normal life to an immediate end. "And there is movement." I heard those words and knew my life had changed.

It was the Jewish New Year, Rosh Hashanah, when I heard those words, and I wondered what the coming year would be like for me. I knew it was wrong to pray for miracles, but I prayed this disaster would pass me by. I prayed for escape. Above all, I prayed for strength, to survive whatever happened, to absorb it all and not pass on the emotional turmoil to my children or my mother.

But the legal pirouette had begun, and my lawyer and Gillen agreed to meet.

I had been represented, from the very earliest days of the Iran/Contra affair, by W. DeVier Pierson. Pierson was a Johnson Democrat, now sixty, who had originally come to Washington from his native Oklahoma to work for Senator Mike Monroney of that state. He had been recruited to join Johnson's White House staff in 1967 and had been Special Counsel to the President. He had left the White House, and the federal government, in 1969, and had founded a law firm in Washington that concentrated on energy matters. He had become prominent in this specialty, and well off, but like the best men with this background he longed for the excitement and the moral rewards of the old days in government. He had been interested in the Iran/Contra matter and had even thought of being chief counsel to the Senate Democrats when their investigation began.

It wasn't my idea that Pierson and I should come together. As the Iran/Contra affair began, I had no intention of getting a lawyer. I thought the State Department's Legal Adviser's Office would advise me or anyone else in the Department who sought help. I understood that if someone were targeted for indictment he would have to get his own lawyers, for his interests and those of the Department would diverge, perhaps even conflict. But in the early stages, when not one of us was a target, why would the Department's lawyers not help those who sought help?

The answer was simple: Judge Walsh would not allow it. Privately his people sometimes acknowledged that it would be much harder to pressure and intimidate a witness with counsel. Thus, Department lawyers were not permitted to accompany any official to a meeting with them. Fine, I thought; officials will all refuse to appear without a lawyer, and there will be no meetings. But the White House, wishing to avoid a battle with the newly anointed Walsh, caved in. Department lawyers were to be unavailable: you were on your own. A sense of abandonment by the White House, of being thrown to the wolves, was inevitable.

While this bothered me as a matter of principle, I did not think of it as a practical problem for myself. I had done nothing wrong, and I

UNDUE PROCESS

did not need a lawyer, even in what was turning out to be a great scandal. Thus I blissfully continued for many weeks after the scandal broke, until one Sunday morning by friend Leonard Garment, one of Washington's preeminent lawyers and a veteran of the Watergate scandal, called me up. Come over to my house, he said. Now. I followed orders and showed up fast. I told him generally what I had done and what I had not done, how I had known Oliver North, and what I thought would happen. He asked if I had a lawyer. I answered: "I don't need a lawyer. I haven't done anything wrong."

Garment smiled, then chuckled, then shook me verbally, asking: "Do you hear what you just said to me? Are you listening to yourself talk? You're in the middle of a huge scandal, people are resigning all over the place, you're a lawyer, and you're saying to me, 'I don't need a lawyer because I didn't do anything wrong.' "

I took the point and quickly called Harry McPherson. I had worked for Harry's firm during my brief stint as a Washington lawyer in 1979 and 1980. I very much wanted him to represent me. He was a Washington mover-and-shaker, a Democrat (in fact, Pierson's predecessor as Special Counsel to Johnson), and a man I trusted and respected greatly. He nearly agreed to do so, but his firm had represented someone else involved in Iran/Contra in an unrelated proceeding, and he could not take me on because of the potential conflict. McPherson and Garment together began to search for someone else to represent me—Garment himself was already representing Reagan's former National Security Adviser, Robert C. "Bud" McFarlane—and McPherson thought of Pierson, his friend and colleague from the Johnson White House.

We had never met. I had never heard of him. We talked once on the telephone and met for breakfast soon thereafter at the Four Seasons Hotel. My immediate thought upon meeting him was that he was a ringer for Jimmy Stewart, and as I came to know him better that impression only deepened. Tall, silver-haired, with the polite and old fashioned manners and speech of a well-bred Oklahoman, he is the central casting Western lawyer who talks slowly and quietly, then exits the room leaving everyone feeling satisfied and friendly, and wondering how it is they have all just agreed to give it up and see things his way.

He said he would take the case and not bill his time. Not at all; it would be pro bono. Over the next several years he was to spend hundreds of hours on my case without charging me for his time. He was acting as a citizen, as an American who felt that what he was doing was the right thing. When, five years later, he was to sit across the table from Lawrence Walsh, another Oklahoman (by adoption, and rather late in life), the contrast between the two men would be striking.

Am I a Target?

B ut for now, Pierson was meeting with Walsh's assistant, Gillen, on September 16.

Gillen told him they'd had a very busy year. They'd collected a great deal of new information. And the result had been that they'd been intensifying their investigation of several people, and I was among them. With the statute of limitations running, this was a critical time.

In fact, the statute of limitations on false testimony or perjury is five years. The first testimony of mine that could possibly interest them had been given on October 10, 1986, so as Pierson and Gillen met for the first time we had exactly twenty-four days to go.

Gillen told Pierson, "Our interest with respect to Abrams is in some statements he made in his testimony." So Pierson had been right: they were abandoning fancy, convoluted conspiracy claims and shooting instead for false statements or discrepancies in testimony, or for information withheld from Congress.

And, Gillen went on, "there is movement" in our ongoing investigation. How much? Enough, he said, so that he could not in good conscience require Abrams's testimony before a grand jury. We'd like to have it, he said, but we couldn't require it.

A strange formulation, that. It is common in criminal matters for prosecutors to say they will not compel the testimony of anyone who is a target of their investigation, meaning someone who will soon be indicted. A designated target will be most likely, on advice of counsel, to take the Fifth and refuse to testify. It is logical: if they've said you're about to be indicted, why take the risk of giving them additional information to use against you? Nothing you say will help you, and something you say might hurt you. So every criminal lawyer will give the same advice: Shut up. Prosecutors could get you to testify by granting immunity from prosecution, of course, but that would defeat their goal; and if they are tricky and tell you there's no danger of indictment when there really is, a judge might throw the case out later on.

So what was Gillen saying? Pierson looked for answers: You've not said Mr. Abrams is a target. Gillen replied that he'd prefer not to use that word, then repeated that he would not compel my testimony, and would not compel the testimony of a target. So, it seemed to me, I was a target but they would not call me one.

Could we supply exculpatory information? Pierson asked. Sure. But, Pierson asked, which types? What are your specific concerns? Oh, that wouldn't be prudent, Gillen replied, wouldn't be prudent to tell you that, show you documents, tell you about specific testimony. But why not? asked Pierson; you've been investigating Mr. Abrams for five years now. How can it be imprudent to discuss what you think he did wrong?

Well, said Gillen, we are searching for the truth. If we give you the questions we have about Abrams's behavior, you'll all sit down and think up answers. We think we'll get a better answer if we require an immediate response. Well, now, Pierson answered, that is really debatable, when the matter here is five years old. Do you really believe that giving him no opportunity whatsoever to think before he answers, about things that happened five years ago, is the best way to get at the truth? And do you think it's fair that his only opportunity to learn your concerns and respond to them comes before the grand jury, where he is obviously in danger?

UNDUE PROCESS

At first I did not see the danger, but my lawyers—for I was soon to have others, in addition to Pierson, working on my case—explained it. These things are all five years old, they said, and you may remember something inaccurately. Or not at all. Later they may show you evidence that proves you answered wrong, and you'll remember better, and correct your answer, but you'll look like a liar to a jury. Don't commit yourself under oath to answers that are made without thought, without reviewing documents, because every later change will impeach your own credibility.

Gillen understood Pierson's point and expressed "empathy" for my problem, but said he was compelled to take that position; he could not give away the ranch.

Pierson sought a compromise. How about an interview? It was a fair proposal: not under oath, but as revealing to them as it would be to me. An equal contest. With my lawyer present. In most jurisdictions in the United States a witness appearing before a grand jury is not entitled to have a lawyer present, because Supreme Court decisions have never extended the Sixth Amendment's guarantee of "assistance of counsel" that far. So despite the obvious fact that the prosecutors have you in the palm of their hand and control the grand jury proceedings lock, stock, and barrel, and your testimony may well endanger your freedom, you have no right to a lawyer. It's a bizarre gap in constitutional protections.

Oh no, said Gillen, an interview is not a satisfactory way to proceed. There's no verbatim transcript. If Abrams has a statement to make, let him make it to the grand jury. Then he'll see all the statements and documents we're using, and you'll know what we're interested in.

Pierson now reminded Gillen of my earlier interviews, which had culminated with Geoffrey Stewart's volunteered assurances that they had been satisfied with my veracity. Gillen didn't deny or debate that point but suggested we look at North's statements before Congress during his Iran/Contra testimony. That material, from 1987, was not new to me or to Pierson, Gillen noted, but was new to the OIC, for they had been forbidden to read it during the North trial. North had received immunity for this Congressional testimony, and as the prosecutors would be unable to use it against him, they had been compelled by law not to listen to it, lest it taint their own case against him. Now, with the North case tried, they had reviewed it. Is that a significant source of information about Abrams? Pierson asked. Well, it's *a* source, anyway, Gillen replied.

Not much of a clue. North had said almost nothing specific about me in that testimony, beyond alleging that just about everyone in the Administration had known what he was up to, including me. Could such a generalized allegation—at one point he suggested that if I had not asked him whether he ran the private network, it must have been because I already knew he did—really mean much?

Pierson gave me his sense of things: this was the old whipsaw, the classic dilemma people can be put in by prosecutors. You're on notice that you appear before the grand jury at some peril, but you are given no other means of finding out what concerns them, no other means of defending yourself. You are in jeopardy if you appear; you are in jeopardy if you stay away. It did not look as though they'd relent here and just grant me an informal interview.

Now, Pierson said to me, he could just go in and present the case: do an oral argument to Walsh, and do a brief. Or I could go ahead and appear before the grand jury. That would show I was not afraid to do so and would smoke out their "evidence." The prosecutors could size me up as a person, and as a witness, and I could respond on the central issues. I would at least know what the charges and the evidence were, without waiting to be indicted. And presumably we could get their agreement that after that grand jury session, Pierson and I could meet with them again and present all the exculpatory evidence—my side of the case.

Very tempting. I wasn't scared of them or their "evidence." I was confident I would impress them as a credible person and a powerful witness. Either they would believe me and drop the case, or they would conclude that they would lose their case if they brought it to trial. They'd see they could never convince a jury beyond a reasonable doubt that I had known North was running the private network or, for that matter, that he was doing anything illegal. Two hours on the stand, and this terrible business would be over.

It made sense, logically and emotionally. I was certain of the facts, certain of my ability as a speaker, and certain I could never be indicted. I was a lawyer, a former Assistant Secretary of State; more important, I was *me*. I wasn't the kind of person who gets indicted. It was ridiculous. It was impossible. The very word "indictment" made me cringe, in the same way many people cringe when they hear the word "cancer." I never used it. I said they might "go against me" or "move against me" or "move ahead." Guys on the evening news got indicted, guys holding raincoats over their faces, guys in handcuffs, guys with forty million dollars in seventeen secret bank accounts. Not me.

But Pierson was smarter, and less emotional. That's why you hire a lawyer. He too was tempted by the idea of an appearance before the grand jury, but, he told me, he was not a criminal lawyer. It was time to get a more experienced judgment. Did I know any criminal lawyers I could call?

Not really. I knew a few, but not well, not as friends. The best idea was to call Len Garment. Fine, said Pierson; call him today, ask him to pledge confidentiality, and ask his advice. Garment had represented Bud McFarlane. He would know the ropes.

I called him. Garment was a man of sparkling wit who threw puns and jokes and wisecracks faster than you could catch them. But when you had a problem, when you were in trouble, he was the confidant and counselor you wanted: the humor did not disappear, it fortified advice composed of prudence, experience, and legal shrewdness. He listened silently as I went through the facts and told him I now had to decide whether to appear. I had to figure out, that is, whether such an appearance could really diminish the chances of an indictment. Tough call, he said. It sounds like they will indict you if you don't appear. It's a bad sign they won't talk to you except before the grand jury. At least theoretically, you still might be able to turn them around. The risks don't seem too high, at least not dispositive. But, he added, let me tell you what most criminal lawyers will tell you: don't do it. And you should talk to some criminal law experts. Soon.

New Lawyers

The next day, September 17, Pierson and I showed up at Garment's office and were introduced to Barry Levine and Peter Morgan. Both were Garment's law partners, both criminal law experts.

Morgan was not what I expected in a criminal lawyer. He had just returned to the firm after two years of teaching at a law school, had recently completed a massive law review article on the political uses and abuses of the false testimony statute, and was a former English lit major with a razor-sharp intellect. A thoughtful type, he had more of the air of the literary intellectual about him than of the criminal lawyer, and his black-framed glasses only added to the effect.

Levine seemed to me the quintessential criminal lawyer, far more emotional, far more aggressive. He resisted sitting still, often lifted in midsentence by the sheer force of his own energy. Waiting for others to finish their sentences was a burden, and he interrupted Garment often enough to elicit an occasional "Let me finish for once!" He looked like a former athlete who was still in shape, a bantamweight still ready to go ten rounds. And indeed he was a fighter. Just as a certain type of doctor becomes a surgeon, and just as surgeons love to cut, criminal lawyers love to fight. He viewed Walsh's office as a menace to society—riddled with bad intentions and rotten tactics—and for the best reason: not political, not ideological, but because they were after *me*. He was instantly on my team, he *was* my team before I knew I had one or needed one, and while I sat wondering if those might be Indians over that next hill, he was circling the wagons and piling up ammunition.

Morgan and Garment were familiar with the Iran/Contra case generally through the firm's representation of McFarlane; Levine was not. The McFarlane case was long over, but could there be a conflict? Could the firm represent Bud, and me, too? Not at the same time, but McFarlane no longer needed legal representation. He would unquestionably waive any possible conflicts; if worse came to worst, he would probably agree to use a different lawyer if some new problem arose, some new need for his testimony. More to the point, he had left the Reagan Administration very soon after I had taken the Latin America job, so in fact we had never worked together. There was virtually no overlap in our activities, and, again, his case was closed. So, we felt, there could be no possible conflict in having the firm represent me.

Should I testify before the grand jury? The "pro" points were clear. I should use any fair opportunity to avoid indictment. I would present myself well and would deal well with any new information. And I would learn what, if any, new information they thought they had against me from North's notebooks or the more recent grand jury testimony he had given in 1991, as a witness with immunity, after his conviction. And there was an emotional argument as well: they were after me. They were shooting at me. I wanted to *do* something, to defend myself, to act, to engage them. Not just by hiring lawyers, not just indirectly. Myself. Face to face. What could be wrong with all that?

Well, the problem of surprise. They show you something, and you can't say "give me a while to think about this." You have to answer, fast. If, later, you decide you don't like that instant answer—you remember something new, or different—you're dead. Now you're changing your answer. Now you have a credibility problem. And before you know it, they have additional counts against you.

UNDUE PROCESS

Look, Levine said, why do they want you before the grand jury, why do they refuse to allow an informal interview? Simple. To trap you. To trap you into instant positions where you may not put your best foot forward. They don't want to give you a chance to exculpate yourself, which an interview would do; they want to give you a chance to trap yourself.

But, I asked, what if they believe me?

They don't believe you, he replied. They don't and they won't. If they believed you, you wouldn't be here today. They are trying to force you to deal with new evidence at the point and in the manner where you are weakest and least able to do so. They want your untutored reaction to this new stuff, and later, you're locked in. You are under oath, and you can't defend yourself later against off-the-cuff answers you have given.

Listen to me, he said. There are *no* gains from going before the grand jury. None. Just this kind of grand jury testimony will end up as new counts in the indictment. You have *no* chance of persuading them of your credibility. If they are in doubt about that, if they want to meet you, they can do that without the grand jury. They won't.

Remember, he said, there really is no such thing as a grand jury, in the terms we're talking about. The audience is the prosecutors only. Not the grand jurors. And the prosecutors have already made up their minds that you are a criminal. What the grand jurors think is not relevant, not in real life.

I knew that was true. I had testified three times before the grand jury, and it had shocked me. Somehow I had gotten out of law school believing the grand jury was a protection for citizens. Prosecutors couldn't just indict people; they had to persuade the grand jury to indict. There were standards. There was fairness. This was a procedural protection for citizens.

False. All of it. The grand jurors, when I testified to them, were a mixed crowd of blacks and whites, men and women, young and old. But they were not listening, most of them. Some napped. The prosecutors, as always, asked the questions, drew the conclusions, made the decisions. The grand jury simply rubber-stamped them. In fact it was worse than that, because you were not allowed to have your lawyer there. You were on your own. Somehow the great Warren Court, extending the Constitutional right to counsel all along the criminal process, had missed the grand jury.

So forget the grand jury, Levine said. You have one audience, the prosecutors. And their reviews are already in.

On the other hand, he said, the case sounds spongy. They are not behaving as if they were confident. And they seem to be relying on North, whom they say and believe is a liar. Is he going to be their star witness? A witness they themselves must argue is not credible?

So what do we do? Pierson asked. Should we try the interview route again? Should we appeal to Walsh? Should we submit a brief?

Do everything, Garment answered. Do the maximum. If the case is on edge, it just might help. You never know. The only downside is, you reveal your defense, but it's pretty obvious anyway. Put your best foot forward and show them you have energy, you plan to fight. And appeal to Walsh's sense of fairness and to his, and the staff's, desire to avoid a case that might appear vindictive and political. Let's argue all this to Walsh.

Right, said Morgan. And Elliott should meet with Walsh too. After all, this entire crew was new—Gillen and his boys—and had never even met me. Walsh had seen me once for ten minutes. But let's not do a factual presentation to them; that would reveal our case and would not win them over. You can't prove a negative, and you'll never prove to them what Elliott didn't know on a given day.

So we decided: we would go back and appeal to the OIC again, tell them that what they were asking me to do was unconscionable. How can you impose the peril of the grand jury to ask about events five years old? Meanwhile, Pierson said to me, get to work. Start reading your testimony, all of it, again. Read all the relevant depositions and testimony by others. Review your notes of your previous grand jury appearances.

Homework. And I felt just as my kids do when the teacher gives them a big assignment in the subject they like least. Did I really have to read it all *again,* for the ninety-third time? Did I have to bathe in it again, now, five years later? I did. What did I know and when did I know it? Who are the witnesses? When did I learn this? Why did I say

UNDUE PROCESS

that? When did I hire A? When did B move on? Why did I call Alan Fiers on that Monday in September 1985?

I approached the task with a small feeling of desperation, a large dose of boredom, and overwhelming resentment. It was like one of those dreams where someone is chasing you but you can't seem to run away. I seemed unable to get the calendar to move; somehow it was always September 1985, and I could not get away.

I went home early that day, September 17, 1991, because that evening was the beginning of Yom Kippur, the holiest day in the Jewish calendar, a day of fasting and prayer. I went to synagogue with my wife that evening and returned for seven hours the next day. I prayed, again, for strength. I prayed for a good year. I prayed that whatever happened to me, God would continue to shower on me the true blessings He had given me: the health and happiness of my wife and my children.

"Perjury, False Testimony, Obstruction of Justice"

On September 18, Wednesday, Yom Kippur, Pierson spoke to Gillen once again. He asked Gillen to reconsider his demand that I go before the grand jury, arguing the equities. These events were five years behind us; was it really fair to ask for instantaneous responses? He noted that I wanted to appear, but no lawyer worth his salt would let me, after thinking it all through.

Well, said Gillen, we have documents to show him, documents from those days in the mid-1980s; we want to pin him down. That's the point, Pierson replied; you have five-year-old documents, and it isn't fair, it's a trap, to ask him about them with no time to think. That's precisely why he can't appear. He isn't going to appear before the grand jury. Period.

Gillen didn't debate the point; he said he'd think about it, talk to others on the staff, think about other approaches. Well, if you can't give us any relief on this, Pierson said, I'd like to put this argument to Judge Walsh directly; could you set up an appointment for me? Yes, said Gillen, and I'll call you back tomorrow.

Pierson reported this all to me Thursday morning, September 19.

Gillen had dropped a few hints. He had mentioned North a few times—his testimony and some documents. Pierson had asked if that included the North notebook, and Gillen had answered "certainly." I had never read North's notebook but had heard from others who had read it that references to me in it were sparse. A prominent figure in the congressional Iran/Contra hearings had told me the notebooks proved North had *not* trusted me, had withheld information from me, had viewed me as "Shultz's boy." But we had to try to obtain and read the notebooks, and see just when and how I appeared in them.

Gillen had also mentioned the magic triangle: North had been convicted and had gotten off only because of the immunity issue; Alan Fiers had now confessed; and that left Abrams. Was this guilt by association? Pierson had asked him. No, no, Gillen had said, we have documents indicating the link between them.

Now that was an old story, the story of the RIG and the RIGlet. When I had taken over the Latin America bureau at State in July 1985, everyone had told me it was critical to maintain close relations with the other bureaucracies, with the guys I'd be working with: NSC, CIA, DOD. So I had continued the practice my predecessor had begun of holding a weekly meeting of the people running Latin American affairs in those agencies, perhaps a dozen in all. Among them were usually Alan Fiers for CIA and Oliver North for the NSC, though neither ever came alone. We called this group of ten or fifteen the Restricted Interagency Group or RIG. And it was just plain ridiculous to argue that illicit activities had been mentioned, much less planned, at its meetings.

First of all, several attendees had kept notes. No doubt those notes had come into the hands of the prosecutors years before, and they would show the truth: that we had all spent endless hours trying to make sure no illegal activities ever took place, trying to make sure that we kept within the gerrymandered, constantly changing borders of the Boland Amendment.

Second, the attendees were available to testify, and no doubt had testified, to what happened at those meetings, and they would confirm what the contemporaneous notes showed.

Third, among the attendees were people from four different bureaucracies, generals and admirals, colonels, civil servants, lawyers;

the idea that the RIG had ever winked at illegal activity was prepos-
terous.

Finally, there were simply too many people there to conspire ef-
fectively.

Aha, said the prosecutors, as had the Congressional investigators
before them, but the RIG was a sham; the real decisions were made by
the trio of Abrams, North, and Fiers in what came to be called the
RIGlet. After a RIG meeting, before one, outside of one, you three met
and exchanged secrets and called the shots.

So the account went, but it was false. We three had met, alone,
without the presence of others, a total of three or four times in the
sixteen months I had led the bureau before the scandal erupted and
North was fired. At all other times we met in larger groups, or with at
least one other person present. The RIGlet was a construct of conspiracy theorists.

But here it was again, this time from Gillen. His claim to have
documents showing that the trio of North, Fiers, and Abrams made the
key decisions was false, I knew. Moreover, he surely knew by now
that Fiers and North had shared explosive secrets that they had kept
from me, above all the fact that Iranian money had been diverted to the
Contras.

What were the crimes they thought I had committed? Pierson had
asked Gillen. Can you at least tell us that? Yes: perjury, false testimony, obstruction of justice.

Obstruction of justice? Was he serious? I would as readily have
expected to be accused of bank robbery. When? How? And what false
testimony? What perjury? Gillen had not specified. But he had added
that I had not only misled the Congress; I had also "misled the American people" in comments I had made in an appearance on the Evans
and Novak television show on October 10, 1986. Great, I thought; a
new crime. Maybe they'll call it "conspiracy to hoodwink Evans and
Novak." Gillen had admitted that what I had said to Evans and Novak
did not necessarily constitute a crime, but he didn't like it; it showed
somehow that I had known my statements to Congress were false, and
that I had intended to mislead.

I wondered what he could possibly be talking about. On the one hand, he obviously had in mind, had no doubt already drafted, a multicount indictment. The false testimony count would be in violation of Title 18 of the United States Code, Section 1001:

> Whoever, in any matter within the jurisdiction of any department or agency of the United States knowingly and willfully falsifies, conceals or covers up by any trick, scheme, or device a material fact, or makes any false, fictitious or fraudulent statements or representations, or makes or uses any false writing or document knowing the same to contain any false, fictitious or fraudulent statement or entry, shall be fined not more than $10,000 or imprisoned not more than five years, or both.

Historically, Section 1001 and its predecessors had been used to punish submission of false data—usually false financial data—to agencies of the Executive Branch of the government. The Supreme Court decided in 1955 that this old false statement law would henceforth also be applied to statements to Congress and the Judicial Branch; but the cases prosecuted under 1001 that involved Congress had continued to revolve around corruption. Rita Lavell had been prosecuted in 1985 for false statements made while at EPA: she had intruded into a case involving her former employer, and then denied having done so. Her statements, however, had been made in writing, signed, and under oath. Representative Charles Diggs had been prosecuted under 1001 in 1978 for false payroll authorization forms filed with the House as part of a salary kickback scheme. And Representative George Hansen had been prosecuted in 1985 for filing false personal financial disclosure forms with the House.

The first case in U.S. history to apply Section 1001 to policy disputes, to unsworn testimony about Administration policy by Executive Branch officials, was U.S. v. Oliver North. Walsh & Co. had invented this. They liked their little innovation and would now try it out on me. It was an interesting theory, but, as the law professors say, it proved too much.

Every time you testify you select what to say and what not to say, which is to say that you withhold information. Historically, countless witnesses—from testimony on the Mexican War in 1848 to Robert McNamara's testimony on the Cuban Missile Crisis and his Gulf of Tonkin testimony on Vietnam in 1964, with innumerable examples before and since—had withheld enormous amounts of information, deliberately creating impressions on Capitol Hill that were entirely wrong. Members of Congress had sometimes gotten mad, but no one until Walsh had ever suggested that such testimony was a crime. A lot of former Cabinet members would still be stamping license plates had that ever been the case before.

But now Judge Walsh had developed his own theory. The selection of facts for testimony before Congress was now to be tested not by political standards, where they had always been weighed, but by courtroom standards. And if Judge Walsh and his staff thought the scales tipped a bit to one side—Boom! Indictment.

The perjury counts they were going to bring, I figured, must relate to my repetition under oath, in 1987 to the Iran/Contra Committees and to the grand jury, of unsworn testimony I had given to Congress in 1986. The testimony hadn't changed, but if they proved it false the penalty would be higher.

The obstruction counts they had in mind were bizarre. The statute, Title 18 of the United States Code, Section 1505, read like something out of *The Untouchables:*

> Whoever corruptly, or by threats or force, or by any threatening letter or communication influences, obstructs, or impedes . . . the due and proper administration of the law . . . or the due and proper exercise of the power of inquiry under which any inquiry or investigation is being had by either House, or any committee of either House, or any joint committee of the Congress shall be fined not more than $5,000 or imprisoned for not more than five years, or both.

I had not "corruptly" done anything, whatever that might mean to Walsh. I hadn't pulled a gun on any congressman. I had shredded no documents. I had not consulted, much less conspired, with anyone over what to say and not to say. No matter, my lawyers explained: the theory will be that you withheld information *because* you wanted to frustrate Congressional inquiry into the scandal. That's corrupt enough for Walsh.

False testimony, perjury, obstruction of justice. I repeated the litany to myself over and over. It was what you threw at some mob boss when he suborned or threatened witnesses in a gangland slaying. It all seemed unreal at first. And it remained unreal. Indictment. Obstruction of justice. 1001. What planet was this?

Pierson brought me back down to earth. He wanted my homework. Do a new chronology of October 1986, he said, with all your meetings, your phone calls, your own notebook entries. Search your records. List the things you *now* know Ollie North knew, and Fiers knew, and you never knew. What precisely did they keep from you? What *did* you know about the private arms supply network, and from what source? When did you realize that some statements of yours were wrong, and what did you do when you found out?

Good questions, but I did not want to answer them. Not *again*. I had testified about this in 1987 to the Tower Commission. Twice. And again to the congressional Iran/Contra committees, for two straight days. And again to the Grand Jury. Three times. And all that had been three and a half, four, five years ago. And now, again? Yup, said Pierson. Again.

"A Prosecutor Can Indict a Ham Sandwich"

By Friday, September 20, normal life had ended. I was supposed to be in the Dominican Republic on business that day, but had canceled the trip. I had canceled lunches scheduled for Monday, Tuesday, and Wednesday of the following week. I had backed out of a black tie dinner for Monday night. I spent my time going to one lawyer's office or another's, and rereading what I had done and said in the fall of 1986. There was no present except the fall of 1986, and the lawyers. On Friday morning I went to see Barry Levine. On Friday afternoon I went to see DeVier Pierson. To sharpen the arguments. To recall details. To ask about procedures.

I still did not believe they would indict me, and Levine suspected I was right. I didn't believe it because I couldn't; it didn't compute, it didn't make sense, it was off the charts. *Me?* Levine had a better reason. He was a former Assistant U.S. Attorney, had dealt with U.S. Attorneys' offices all around the country, and knew how any U.S. Attorney would handle this "case." He would throw it out. He might try to scare you into a plea, but he'd never actually waste the time and money a trial would take. Not on these facts. Not five years later. So

41

there was only one problem: did Walsh's office behave as U.S. Attorneys' offices would?

This was indeed the crux of the problem. U.S. Attorneys had thousands of cases, a real caseload, and served for years. They could balance, make judgments; indeed they had to, given their limited resources. Not every case could be tried, and they had to make choices. *De minimis non curat lex,* the old maxim went: the law does not concern itself with trifles. Especially when you had budget problems. Moreover, if he were ambitious, a U.S. Attorney could make his reputation in many, many ways. Cases came across the transom every day. No one case was make-or-break. And finally, a U.S. Attorney had precedents to follow, from his own office and other U.S. Attorneys' offices, and general guidelines from the Department of Justice. He was not flying solo.

That was, after all, what was meant by law: a code, a rule, a body of rules. Predictable. Established. But here, we were dealing with something different. The OIC had unlimited time, an unlimited budget, no precedents, no effective control from the Justice Department, no counterpart offices, and, for the staff, just one case on which to make or break their ambitions and their reputations. These were young men, men like Gillen, now thirty-nine, who had left his family behind in Atlanta. He had gotten his B.A. at the University of North Carolina and his law degree from Emory University in Atlanta, and had been a prosecutor since the day he left law school. He had toiled in obscurity for a decade on organized crime cases and drug enforcement task forces, and now he had his chance for a day in the sun. Would he make his reputation by telling people, ''Wow, what a time I had in Washington! You wouldn't believe the cases I declined! You wouldn't believe the restraint I exercised!''? Would he impress people by showing them the empty pages in his scrapbook? No. He would make his reputation by indicting. By getting scalps. Like mine.

And that is what worried all of us. There is an old New York saying: ''A prosecutor can indict a ham sandwich if he wants to.'' True, but he usually doesn't want to. Because around the corner there is a drug dealer to indict, a man who stole one hundred million dollars to prosecute, a murderer to put away. For Walsh and company, around the corner was . . . going home. Obscurity. Boredom. Was I the ham sandwich?

We had a decision to make. We had all agreed I would not appear before the grand jury. Now, should I do an interview with Walsh's office? Not under oath, and no transcript. Just an interview, but with FBI agents present, taking notes, and doing "302s." Form 302 is the agent's report of an interview. If it were important enough in a later trial, he could be called in to testify about what his notes meant and what I had said. So there was risk for me, almost the same risk that arose from going before the grand jury. Of course, my lawyers would be there, and there would be no exact transcript, but the point was the same: they wanted to show me evidence in a context where my chances to think, to remember, would be minimized, and my problems and risks would be maximized.

But could I not persuade them I was telling the truth, could I not win them over? What were my chances? I asked Levine.

None, he said. None. Okay, I said. So we all agreed, no interview. That afternoon, Pierson and Morgan trooped over to tell Gillen.

Pierson reported to me on the following Monday, September 23. Gillen had not complained about our decision on the interview. But a problem had arisen: both Gillen and Walsh were concerned about my lawyers.

Levine, Morgan, and Garment were members of the firm called Dickstein, Shapiro & Morin, and the firm—and indeed two of them as individuals—had represented McFarlane. This was a conflict, Gillen had said. Morgan had told Gillen there was no conflict, and anyway they were simply counseling me on a preindictment basis. Oh no, Gillen had said, it's a very fundamental problem. But both clients, both Abrams and McFarlane, will gladly sign a waiver, Morgan had said. But we won't, Gillen had replied. Pierson had told Gillen: Look, I precipitated this, I advised Elliott to get the advice of some criminal lawyers, to get a second opinion. That advice should not now prejudice his interests. Gillen had replied he'd talk to Walsh about it again.

On the case itself, Pierson had once again pressed Gillen for something more specific. What was the problem? What statements, what conduct? Abrams had testified a thousand times. What concerned them? I'm not prepared to give you that, Gillen had said; the investigation is on-going. Pierson had replied strongly: this was simply, plainly, unfair. How am I supposed to advise my client, how is he supposed to review his testimony, when you won't give us the slightest idea what you think he has done wrong? Well, Gillen had responded, I'm not going to give you the specific statements or actions, but I'll call you tomorrow and tell you some general areas. And if you plan to see Judge Walsh and make a presentation to him, it should be this week. Time is running out. Next Friday is the 27th.

This was Friday night. I had a Little League game to attend, then a party—at Len Garment's house, a book party honoring my friend and his, Gertrude Himmelfarb. Rachel and I would attend. So would Levine and Morgan, so she would meet them. At last.

I went to the game, sat in the stands with the other parents, found I was not seeing anything. The material world had ceased to exist, because *it,* the case, was the only thing that existed. I waved to my ten-year-old son, Jacob, and watched him play, but only for a few minutes. I could not sit there. I wanted to get to the Garments' house, to get back with the lawyers. To the only real world. Rachel came to the game, having dropped our nine-year-old daughter, Sarah, at *her* Little League game, which she now had to return to. We arranged a ride home for our son, Rachel went back to our daughter's game, and I went home. I had watched the game for ten minutes. I changed, shaved, and then went on to the party.

Nice party, if you are about to be indicted. People I knew, people who knew me, old friends, acquaintances. Dick Cheney. Lynne Cheney. Justice Scalia. Katherine Graham of the *Washington Post.* George Will. Larry and Ricky Silberman, she working on Clarence Thomas's confirmation, he now a Court of Appeals judge. What do you say to them? You say, Hi, how are you? And talk about Clarence Thomas. It was almost funny, this feeling of "I've Got a Secret"; almost, but not quite. I felt like an impostor, someone in disguise, a secret agent.

Then Morgan and his wife arrived, and soon Levine, and we began to talk. Levine had some things to say. I knew a trial would cost a fortune. What if I run out of money? I asked Levine again. What if I can only raise half of your fee? I won't leave you, Levine said. Walsh doesn't want me in this case, but I'll be in it, and I intend to beat him. I'll go through to the end with you. It is possible, I thought, that he doesn't know what it means for me to hear him say that. It feels like the sun has just come out from behind a cloud and is beginning to warm me up.

Now, about a plea bargain, he went on. Depends on the plea. If you plead to a crime of moral turpitude, you'll be disbarred. Now the dark cloud was coming back, and I felt the chill again. Why were people saying these things to me, I wondered? Saying words like "disbarred" and "crime" and "jail"? Stop! I was just chatting with Dick Cheney and his wife and you just said "disbarred" to me, so now you must leave the planet. Sorry, but rules are rules.

One more thing, Levine said. Once you start down this plea bargain road, they know you are willing to plead, and who knows where you'll end up. The "slippery slope" argument, familiar to all lawyers, applied here too. You might decide to plead to X, but they draw you along, step by step, no one step big enough to cause you to throw over the whole thing and go to trial. Watch out.

Levine was ready for a trial, but he was trying very hard to show me all sides of the issue. Listen, he said, a trial would be a real test. The government will try, not as a by-product but as a deliberate strategy, to break your spirit and your resources. This will be horrible. And look, if you plead to some Mickey Mouse crap without moral turpitude, without disbarment, you can go on with your life. Life would be better, God knows, without the taint of the plea, without the conviction, but you would overcome it. You would.

I know, I told him. Rachel and I have talked about it, and we know the difference between all of this and real tragedy, like somebody dying or getting cancer. Levine agreed; he knew what real tragedy was, and said, You will survive. Life has to go on. It will go on. You are forty-three. You have three kids. You'll get through this.

Rachel arrived and met Levine and Morgan, whom she took to immediately. But Barry Levine was the true kindred spirit for her, more than Pierson or Morgan. She didn't think he was smarter or a better lawyer, that wasn't it; he was a prize fighter. He was outraged;

he wanted to beat the crap out of Walsh in the courtroom. That was what attracted her, for it was what she felt too.

We all talked for hours, staying on when the other guests had left. What next, what now? Perhaps I should call Secretary Shultz and ask him to write to Walsh, telling Walsh that the accusation I lied to Congress was an accusation I had lied to him as well, and he rejected it. And would so testify. If they were on the line, and couldn't decide whether to indict, maybe the thought of Shultz on the witness stand would affect the decision.

We spoke briefly about fundraising, about how I might raise a million bucks, if the bastards went through with it. When they talked about negotiations, pleas, agreements, and compromises, Rachel bridled. Her situation was worse than mine, for if I was almost powerless here, almost unable to determine my fate over the next day, week, or year, she was even more so. She wanted to fight this evil. Lawyers who wanted to be reasonable were the enemy. She told them, with her tone of voice and her expression, what she thought of their neat, careful distinctions and their lawyerly manner. But they are the best, they are on my side, I thought. *My* lawyers. My team. It didn't help, and I knew why. Because it was happening to me, only to me. They would each go back to their lives; this was my life. The entire sense of unfairness, the savage sense of abandonment, all of it concentrated on them, just because they were there and it wasn't happening to them.

"If He Had to Give Up North, He Needed a New Conviction"

On Tuesday, September 24, Pierson called to tell me of a telephone conversation with Gillen. Walsh had agreed to see Pierson on Thursday the 26th at 2:30 P.M. But he would see *only* Pierson. What? How could that be, I wondered? Don't I even get to choose my lawyers? Walsh felt very strongly, indeed was adamant, on the conflict of interests issue. He felt it was clear, not a close call.

What in hell was going on? This wasn't a trial, it was giving me advice, privately, confidentially. Couldn't I have who I wanted for that? I thought back to 1987, when Walsh had prevented State Department officials from having the help of State's Legal Adviser's Office. This was getting to be a pattern: they don't fight with your lawyers, they try to stop you from having lawyers, or the lawyers you want or can afford.

I was angry, and I knew what was going on here. Walsh connected Garment and his firm with McFarlane all right, and was bitter about the losses they had dumped in his lap in the McFarlane case. McFarlane had pleaded to misdemeanor counts, no felonies, and once Garment had persuaded Walsh to accept that, a ceiling had been set. Henceforth

47

Walsh would never get anyone to plead to a felony. No doubt he felt he had been outmaneuvered, and the fact that Garment was the one to have outsmarted him did not make things any easier.

More recently McFarlane, with Barry Levine by his side, had shot the North case dead. North had been convicted, but his conviction had not been upheld on appeal. The Court of Appeals had bought North's "taint" argument, the proposition that his testimony before the Iran/ Contra Committees, testimony that was not supposed to be used against him in any way, had possibly influenced witnesses in his trial. The case had been remanded to the District Court for further hearings on precisely this point. And then McFarlane had testified, on September 13, that he had bathed in North's congressional testimony, had watched it religiously, never missed a split second, and it had all made a deep impression on him. A profound impression. It had unquestionably influenced his testimony at the North trial. Bang! North was free. Within days after the McFarlane testimony, Walsh had been forced to drop the case against North, his biggest fish, his most valuable conviction. And he no doubt bitterly resented what McFarlane had done, and just as bitterly resented the lawyers who had helped him do it— who were now, some of them, my lawyers.

It was at that moment that I understood North and I might be opposite sides of the same coin to Walsh: if you had to turn one face of the coin down, the other would come up. If he had to give up North, had given up North, he needed a new face. Mine. He needed a new conviction. Editorial comment after he had given up on the North case had been fierce. Five years and fifty million dollars, and nothing to show for it. Laughing stock. Loser. Oh, yes, he needed another scalp once he had lost Ollie's. And it looked as though it would be mine.

So I took a deep breath and forced myself to realize how deadly serious this was going to be. Levine might have been right that no U.S. Attorney would ever, ever bring a case like this; but Walsh was not a U.S. Attorney. Just then, just then did I begin to think: My God, they may actually do this. And as a starter, as a first shot, they were telling me I could not have the lawyers I wanted to represent me.

The sheer, absolute injustice of it was a deep wound. It was no technical matter to me. I had come to feel I was in deep water, and the hands being stretched out to keep me afloat were of greater and greater emotional importance. Barry Levine was a fighter, and his tough attitude toward Walsh was an emotional tonic to me and to my wife. And now Walsh wanted us to do without that tonic, that nourishment. For the first time, I experienced a feeling of hatred for those people. It was no longer politics, the reflexive conservative opposition to Walsh's office—it was personal. They were not playing fair. They were trying to screw me, any way they could.

And we were powerless. If we had been in court, if we ever got to court, they could bitch and moan about my lawyers, but there would be a real judge—not Judge Walsh—deciding whether they would be disqualified. At that moment, however, we needed to curry favor with Walsh and Gillen. A confrontation with them over this issue was crazy. Even if they backed off, it would create resentment and bad feelings, and it was possible that their resentment of Garment and his firm would rub off on me. It was imprudent to push this issue, the lawyers all agreed. Imprudent. Unwise. Those miserable dirty sons of bitches, I thought; they won't even let me have my lawyers.

I had already found that when you were threatened with indictment, you had two lifelines: your lawyer and your wife. In a world suddenly out of control, you clung to them and trusted no one else. When months later I learned that Walsh had subpoenaed both Oliver North's wife and his lawyer Brendan Sullivan to appear before the grand jury, I understood what he was up to: he was trying to break those lifelines. Oh, you can assert the lawyer-client privilege and the spousal privilege, and they need not testify in the end, but Walsh and his team must have known what they were about. Besides the cost in time and money, both inexhaustible for Walsh and in short supply for his target, this was pure intimidation. The goal was to isolate the target, to break his spirit, to raise doubts in his mind as to whether any person or relationship was truly safe from the prosecutors' might. All prosecutors could do this; few ever sank so low.

There was another issue on the table, Pierson had told Gillen: what are the specific areas you are concerned about? Oh yes, Gillen had said, I'll send over a list of those tomorrow, Wednesday the 25th, so you can address them when you see Judge Walsh.

Now, said Pierson, we really had work to do. Was my homework finished? I should devote all day to it, and tomorrow, and we should all meet, the whole legal team, Thursday morning. We had to hone our arguments, come up with the best examples: why I was different from North or Fiers or McFarlane, what I had not known, why pursuing me after five years was unfair, how I had carefully kept the Secretary of State informed whenever I thought there might possibly be an illegal activity taking place. We had to marshal all the exculpatory evidence: National Security Adviser John Poindexter telling North he had kept information from me, North and Fiers never telling me about the Iran connection, the specific occasions when I told Shultz I had found out about or even suspected funny business. We were going to have a shot at Walsh, and we had better be ready.

And now I faced another kind of decision. On Wednesday, September 25, I had a lunch scheduled with a friend from the diplomatic community. Should I go ahead with it? On Thursday the 26th I had an important breakfast to attend in New York. An important client of mine was going to be there, a private consulting client whose fees were very important to my annual income, and he expected to see me. Could I go to New York, or did I have to stay with the lawyers? And on Friday the 27th, the Washington Chapter of the American Jewish Committee was meeting for a luncheon at which I would be elected to the chapter's Board of Trustees. How could I let them go ahead with that, when just a few days later I might be indicted?

My legal problems were devouring my life. All I did during the day was work with the lawyers, work for the lawyers on my records and transcripts, think about what might lie ahead. At night, social life was gone—who was in the mood? At all hours my mother, or my wife's parents, or some friend close enough to be in the know, might call, or one of my lawyers might, and I had to be there. It was all-consuming.

I could not have lunch with my friend. I could not go to New York. I could not let the American Jewish Committee elect me to its Board. I had never truly believed I was going to be indicted, still could not believe it. But now it all had a new reality, because the prospect of it, the fear of it, was starting to infect my life.

It was at this point that I became phone-shy. It had happened once before, briefly, during the Iran/Contra scandal, when each day brought a new newspaper story attacking me. You never knew who was calling, back then, with what "revelation," with what charge, with what accusation. I had come to wince each time the phone rang.

Now, here it was again. When the phone rang my pulse jumped a beat, and if it was one of the lawyers on the phone, my breathing stopped for a second. What was it? Indictment? Some horrible new complication? Given what had already happened, who could rule *anything* out? Pierson seemed to sense it, for he would often begin calls by saying, Hello, I don't have anything new, or, Hello, there's nothing new but I have a question for you. The feeling of dread one has when the telephone rings at 4 A.M.—that "Who died?" reaction—I now felt every time it rang.

Our three children were ten, nine, and six years old. What should we tell them? What did they know? Clearly they knew something was up. My hours had changed, and much more to the point my mood had changed. The phone rang at odd hours and I spent hours on it. For the moment we told them nothing: it was too soon. What was there to tell them, after all? If it all went away, it would have been foolish even to try explaining it. If I were indicted, there would be time enough to tell them.

There were only two alternatives: indictment, or a decision by Walsh not to indict. A guilty plea was not a possibility. I ruled it out. I did not want to hear what I might plead guilty to, how it might work. It was just plain unthinkable to me.

And even more so to Rachel. If I reacted with amazement to the entire affair, with occasional bewilderment, even bemusement, and less often anger that it could be happening, she reacted with rage. And outrage. And that meant that if they wanted a fight, if they would not back off, she thought we should give them one. Fight to the end. Never compromise with those bastards.

What did that mean, fight to the end? That is a question I had asked, at least in the temporal and financial sense. Peter Morgan was direct: a trial would be complicated, lots of pretrial motions. It would take a year before it was all over. Figure on legal fees around a million dollars.

I was only short about $950,000, I figured. But maybe we could raise the money. North had. I was not North, but Walsh was more discredited now, and I would be able to get contributions. Who could tell how much I might raise? What if I couldn't raise enough? Levine was emphatic: I won't desert you. I won't start this, then leave it; I'll finish it. Count on me.

"It" was now virtually the sole topic of conversation between Rachel and me, except for those moments when we stopped to discuss the kids and my mother. How much should we tell her?

When I told my mother I might be indicted, she reacted with agony; my brother, Franklin, wondered if it had been so smart to tell her. But she would find out the hard way if it happened; shouldn't we prepare her? But how much?

The children kept us sane. You cannot truly stop living if you have three children who need cereal and chocolate milk, who need to be picked up and to be delivered, who have homework to do, and who want to have bedtime stories read to them.

But between us, "it" was what Rachel and I talked about. What was happening. What was next. What to tell whom. Whom to trust. What would we do, If.

I felt, more and more each day, that in the Milky Way Galaxy, in the solar system, on the planet Earth, in Washington D.C., the only irreducible unit, the true molecular structure, was Rachel and me. The two of us. Everyone, everything else was outside, more or less. You had to decide what to tell them, when. There might be things you did not want to tell them. Or tell them right then. But at the center, there we were. So I was not alone, never felt alone, not for a single second, and I never wondered what Rachel felt. I knew. She felt, above all, a violent rage at the people who were doing this to her husband. She would have killed them if she could. She would have erased them from the face of the earth without a second thought, and never looked back. She'd have shot Craig Gillen through the heart and gone on to a Little League game. In the best of spirits.

WEDNESDAY, SEPTEMBER 25

"Surely There Was Another Way Out"

After thinking about it, I decided to call Secretary Shultz at Stanford and ask him to write that letter to Walsh. But Shultz reminded me of an old fight he had had with Walsh while Secretary; Walsh had accused him of withholding documents, had attacked him, had said he was obstructing the investigation. I'll be happy to write, Shultz said, but I worry that a letter from me to Walsh would hurt you, not help you. He urged me to talk this over with Abe Sofaer, who had been the Department's Legal Adviser, was a former federal judge, and had a good relationship with Walsh. Maybe he could help. I reached Sofaer on a trip, and he said he would be glad to see if he could help. He'd be back in Washington Sunday. We should talk then. From what he knew of the case, there should be no criminal action here. Surely there was another way out.

Surely we could all find some noncriminal way out. Instead of a fine, I make an equivalent donation to charity. Instead of being sentenced to community service, I volunteer to do it. I make a contrite statement. Something. Where there's a will, there's a way. We could devise something, if Walsh wanted to. If not, if he had to have that scalp, if Gillen's career plans required another human sacrifice, then we'd fight. All the way.

53

THURSDAY, SEPTEMBER 26

"Would You Consider a Disposition?"

On Thursday, September 26, Pierson met with Walsh. Waiting for the readout, I was not tense. This was all still, in some way, an adventure. I was worried, I was excited, I was intensely *involved,* and while walking or driving around I spent my time thinking, exclusively, about *it,* preparing in odd ways for what might be around the corner.

I made up a list of whom to call if I were indicted: clients; people at the Hudson Institute, where I worked; the publisher of the book on U.S. foreign policy I was then completing; relatives. Then I went through my rolodex and made up a list of whom to ask for defense fund money. Rachel made up a separate list from her phone list, and we compared notes. We excoriated the imaginary cheapskates, were grateful in advance to those whom we decided would be generous, decided preemptively never again to speak to those who would simply never call back after the indictment.

We wondered what we would live on, in terms of salary, while the trial was pending. Even if I could raise the defense money, what about normal income? Could I go on a speaking tour? I thought I should write a book and call it *The Elliott Abrams Diet*. The key was the sliding scale of weight loss: you can count on 4 pounds per misdemeanor, 7 pounds per felony, with bonus points if you're actually convicted. I was losing weight steadily by this time, noticing the belts that needed another hole punched in them, the blue jeans that now needed a belt to stay up.

We were at that moment prosperous, with income far exceeding our spending, and a decent amount of cash on hand, so we would enter the trial period comfortably. If a campaign started paying the legal bills, and if the lawyers did not ask for regular, steady payments, we could make it. For a few months, anyway. Then I'd need some new source of income, and thinking about that also took a good deal of time.

But on that Thursday, September 26, Pierson met with Walsh, and for the first time in a while we had hard news. We had some new facts.

Their case was, in essence, quite simple. North was running the Contra arms supply network, and you knew it. You knew it, they said, because North told you, as he told Fiers. And you had enough circumstantial evidence of what he was up to, anyway.

We had worked for long hours on Pierson's presentation, and he reported back that he had been permitted to give it almost uninterrupted. He had spoken for two hours. He had carefully presented my case, and he had taken their case apart. He had reminded them that the National Security Adviser, Robert McFarlane, had flatly told Congress in 1985 that North was not violating any laws. I had relied on that assurance, and had had a right to do so. And North had privately given me, and other colleagues, the same assurance: "I am not breaking the law." Nothing North had said to me, or to the RIG, had revealed an operational role; he knew more than any of the rest of us about the resupply network, but that was part of his job. He gave no hint that he was actually running it. He had carefully hidden from me, to take one very good example, the existence of a secret, encrypted communications net that linked all the parts of his operation.

Moreover, North had numerous times come to me with controversial matters, and I had taken them to Shultz. When, in September 1986, North had wanted to have the U.S. Ambassador in Costa Rica call that country's president to deliver a very strong message, he had called me to ask me to issue the instruction. I had done so, and had reported it to Secretary Shultz. When North had received a message from Panama's Noriega proposing some sabotage in Nicaragua in return for a reduction in U.S. criticism of him, North had asked me what response to give. I had taken it to Shultz, who had rejected the Noriega offer immediately. Pierson gave example after example of this kind of conduct.

There was a pattern here: North had come to me with highly sensitive issues, and I had had reason to believe I understood what he was doing—and not doing. But it was now clear that he and others had kept a good deal from me. North had told Fiers about the arms sales to Iran and the diversion of money to the Contras; he had never said a word about it to me. Poindexter had asked me all about the State Department's effort to help the Contras' finances and had later told North he had carried on this discussion "never letting on we had access to accounts." Neither North nor anyone else had ever informed me of the financial network they had assembled, and North had at times told me, and others in the RIG, that the Contras were starving at moments when he was sitting on million-dollar bank balances. No one had ever told me the Saudi Government was contributing millions to the Contras.

There had been back-channel messages between North and many of the other players, carefully kept from me, and I had never met or heard of North's key operatives, people like Richard Secord and Albert Hakim. While Fiers—according to testimony he gave the Senate Intelligence Committee in the fall of 1991, after his guilty plea—had been told by a superior that denials that North was running the private network were a "charade," neither he nor anyone else had ever said that to me. When Bud McFarlane had told Congress in 1985 that North was running no private network and was strictly abiding by the Boland Amendment, North had told Fiers, "Bud just perjured himself." Neither North nor Fiers nor anyone else had ever said anything similar to me.

No doubt some of this had been kept from me precisely because they all knew I would tell Secretary Shultz, from whom they were carefully concealing it. And the record showed me going to Shultz time after time when sensitive information came in, including the first indications I had—on October 23, 1986—that there had been U.S. Government involvement in the private network. What is more, there were many examples—and Walsh had the notes—of RIG efforts to be sure we stayed within the limits of the law, carefully measuring how far we could and could not go. There had been many meetings with members of Congress, asking them for their guidance on what was legal and what was not.

All in all, Pierson showed in rich detail, there was a clear pattern. I had been told a lot, and *not* told even more. I had not been told the things North and others did not want Shultz to know, for they knew I was reporting to him faithfully and would blow the whistle on any activity that might be illegal or even too close to the line. Above all, I had not been told, nor could I see, that North was actually *running* this private network. I had tried very hard to stay within the confines of the law and to keep my own team at State within them, and had relied on assurances that colleagues in other agencies were doing the same.

Pierson then moved into the policy arguments. The heart and soul of Iran/Contra was the diversion of funds from arms sales to Iran. Every other senior official they had prosecuted had *known* about the diversion; I had not. I had not approved of or participated in violations of the Boland Amendment. I had made misstatements of fact in testimony in October 1986, and no one, not one single person among those who knew all the facts, had come to me and said, Hey, watch it, you've gone too far. When I felt I had gone too far I had tried to set the record straight, and had sought and received permission from Shultz to reveal additional information to the Senate Intelligence Committee.

Now, North's conviction had been reversed, and in all probability Poindexter's would be as well. In view of the end of both of those cases, what was the point of prosecuting me? Was that a sensible exercise in prosecutorial discretion? Wouldn't it seem vindictive, crazy, political, to go after me five years later when much more central figures were to be free of any criminal conviction for their behavior?

UNDUE PROCESS

If they felt I had not met my official responsibilities, they had their final report in which to say so. That was the sensible way to proceed, not just from my point of view, but from theirs as well. They should demonstrate they could exercise restraint in a proper case. They would blunt criticism of their office, and leave a better legacy behind them.

When Pierson finished, Walsh and his team had excused themselves, and had not returned for forty-five minutes. When they had come back, Walsh had told Pierson, you have given us a lot to think about, and we will. But we have a problem. We don't have much time. In two weeks the statute of limitations runs. Would you consider a disposition?

What does that mean? Pierson had asked him. Good question. I'd never heard the expression before, and Pierson now told me it meant a plea bargain. Oh, fuck them, I thought to myself, silently; Pierson was a courtly man and I did not curse in his presence.

Walsh had answered Pierson's question: Oh, something modest, he had said. Like the kind of thing Richard Helms did. Or like Alan Fiers. Alan had something he wanted to get off his chest, and perhaps Elliott does too. We don't just want another scalp, and we are conscious of Elliott's status as a professional man. We could do something that would be "very minimal."

Helms. I knew that Richard Helms, as CIA Director in the 1970s, had withheld something from Congress and had been threatened with perjury charges. He had pleaded guilty to some invented crime, some newfangled use of the contempt of Congress language in section 192 of Title 2 of the U.S. Code. He had waived the contempt citation by the Congress itself and simply pleaded guilty to that misdemeanor, receiving a minimal sentence. What had struck me most about the incident was that as they left the courthouse Helms's lawyer, the legendary Edward Bennett Williams, had said to him, "You can wear this conviction like a badge of honor." But that was in 1977, a political eon ago.

Fiers had just pleaded guilty to the same misdemeanor. None of this was at all relevant to me, I thought, although I didn't much care for Walsh's talking this way. The "professional man" business, Pierson explained, meant that with a misdemeanor plea I wouldn't be disbarred.

Oh, so kind, I thought; so considerate. They said they don't just want another scalp, he reported. How professional. How enlightened.

Well, Pierson had said to Walsh, if you want to do something very minimal, you can use your final report. Right! Independent counsels don't just have the power to indict, they also write reports where they can smear the reputations of people they never indicted. I had long been worried about that, about having Walsh attack me that way, but now it seemed to us the best possible outcome.

We don't view that as a substitute, Walsh had replied. The congressional Iran/Contra committees had a report, and nobody paid any attention to it, and that kind of comment on the situation in a report just isn't satisfactory. Tragic, I thought. Worried your report won't sell well? You will smear people, but no one will know?

But I have no basis for suggesting a disposition like that to Elliott, Pierson had replied. His position, and all the facts at our disposal, all the evidence we have, provide no basis at all for that kind of outcome. We are still shooting in the dark at what concerns you. Given the passage of time, now five years of it, and given the fact that you say you are under the gun because of the statute of limitations, I'm entitled to know what specific statements and evidence you have.

Good answer, I thought. Plead to what? Plead why? We've refuted everything, you'll tell us nothing. Are you relying on testimony from North, whom you've already called a liar? Are you refusing to show us documents because you don't have any? How could Walsh refuse to tell us anything!

He could. Well, we can't do that, he had said to Pierson. I don't see how we can do that.

Then Pierson had asked the sixty-four-thousand-dollar question, the question we had not yet asked. Have you made a decision to indict my client?

No, Walsh had answered, I'm not saying that. We have very substantial concerns. Some kind of disposition of this is going to be necessary. We can't just pass it by. We have no desire to hurt Mr. Abrams. We are not looking for some kind of severe penalty. We can do something very minimal. We can come out with a misdemeanor result. Like the Helms or Fiers cases.

UNDUE PROCESS

But how can I advise my client about all this if I don't know what you are talking about? Pierson had responded.

Well, Gillen had jumped in, we are anxious to see him, and present him with the evidence we have collected. It was he who said no.

Then Pierson had repeated all the arguments he had previously made to Gillen, but this time face to face with Walsh. About fairness. About the five years having elapsed. About the prejudice from confronting evidence five years old, and memories five years old, in front of the grand jury. And Walsh had begun to waver. Hmmmm. Well. Hmmmm.

At which point Gillen had called a recess. The two of them had gone out, and when Walsh returned he had said, No. Sorry. Can't do it.

This was my first inkling of a dynamic I hadn't thought of. I had focused on Walsh, hated him much more than his staff; North had called him a "vindictive wretch," a line I liked. Now it seemed he could be moved, but was being stiffened, being pushed around, by his staff. It made me hate him less. He had wavered over Pierson's fairness argument, had seemed to be responding, and had apparently been overpowered by Gillen. But if I hated him less, I had all the more contempt for him. Here was a man who had been Deputy Attorney General of the United States, president of the American Bar Association, head of one of the top Wall Street law firms—and it looked as if he was letting a thirty-nine-year-old lawyer give him his marching orders.

I sensed the trouble I was in here. Walsh was a zealot, I thought, a legal Calvinist, and this was not politics to him. If I had made a mistake, even if I had apologized for it five years before, I had to be punished. Now. By him. He had been Chosen to chastise the Sinners. As for his staff, they seemed to be Toobin types. Young, aggressive, vicious, political. Either way, I had had it.

Time is running out, Walsh had said. Pierson needed to be in Oklahoma the following week, from September 30 to October 4, and Walsh had been upset on hearing that. Time is running out, and we should resolve this next week, Walsh had said. Then he had added, Your presentation has given us a lot to think about. But we feel strongly about the evidence, and there is evidence you have not covered. I have to tell you, we have a serious matter here. We feel we need to have a disposition of this matter. And if there is a disposition, it will have to include an agreement to cooperate, as in the Fiers case. Please tell Mr. Abrams to think about it.

Now what do I do, I wondered. It was hitting me: my God, my God, they are serious, *they are going to do this to me.* They have heard our side, our brilliant side, our perfect case, and they don't buy it. A "disposition." An "agreement to cooperate."

Peter Morgan, Pierson, and I now thought it through again. There were three options. I could go ahead and do the interview, and then we would all reconnoiter and see where we stood after I had seen their "evidence."

We could negotiate now; of course we could negotiate after the interview just as well, if that was the route we were taking.

Or we could just leave it alone, leave them to make their decision. That was pure Russian Roulette. But maybe all this was just pressure. Maybe Levine's view of the previous week was still correct. Maybe this was just a test to see if I'd fold. Pierson didn't think so; he thought they were serious.

We asked Garment his view, and he added yet another possibility. Maybe they were rushing to judgment here because they were out of time. Maybe we should extend the statute of limitations by one month, so we could all stop for a moment and catch our breath. That would give Walsh time to screw up his courage to the point where he might actually resist his staff. That would show our good faith, and our desire to have all relevant matters considered carefully. But Garment himself said he thought they'd never buy it; they'd reply that they had too many other matters, some dependent on this one, and they had to move ahead.

My head was spinning. Another month of this? My whole life was now organized around the principle that this would be over, one way or another, by October 10. I was literally nauseated by the idea of living with it for an additional month. That way it could drag on, and on, into 1992. It would absolutely destroy the rest of my life, eat it up, crush it.

And when did this business about "negotiate" get into the conversation? Negotiate what? Negotiate becoming a criminal? Negotiate saying "I give up"?

What if they are bluffing? That must be it. Right, I thought. This is a test. I will pass the test. Always darkest before the dawn. This will go away. This is a bad dream, and it will end.

Then Morgan said, this is like the Clair George case. They offered him, his lawyer says, a misdemeanor count to plead to. Plead to a misdemeanor, they said; something minimal, we don't mean to be harsh, etc., etc. George had said no. And they indicted him. They hit him with a ten-count felony indictment. Yeah, Garment said, they're not bluffing. That's what I think, Pierson said. They're not bluffing. I wonder, Morgan said, if they'd take a one count plea to withholding information about the Brunei solicitation, which after all you've already admitted to and apologized for, under 2 USC 192.

Oh.

Ten-count felony indictment, or plead to a misdemeanor. Stand up and say, I'm a criminal.

But just a month ago, a week ago, a minute ago, this was going to go away. It was a bluff. Now, now it was not. I couldn't think clearly. I had that brain fever again from trying to do too many calculations.

Stop. No time for emotions now. What are we analyzing here? There are four factors, the lawyers said. Reputation. Risk of conviction. Expense. And time.

Reputation? Time? Well, a trial could take a year. If you have to appeal, that could be another year. "If you have to appeal," the polite lawyers said. That meant, if you are convicted. If you are convicted of your ten felonies.

Well, what if you are? I said. (What if "you are," not what if "I am.") Morgan answered, fast, without hesitating: "You go to jail." I was speechless. I had read the phrase "he was literally speechless" many, many times. Now I knew what it meant. You had no breath, you could not form words with your breath, and your lips, and your tongue. You see, Morgan explained, there is the sentencing guidelines problem.

Oh God, I thought. What is happening to me? I came in here a normal person and people are talking about jail and sentencing guidelines and my saying, "Yes, Your Honor, I'm a criminal." What is happening to me?

See, Morgan explained, the new federal sentencing guidelines went into effect in November 1986. If you plead guilty to acts committed in October 1986, the guidelines don't apply, and the judge can let you off. With a fine or some community service. But if you are convicted of a felony committed in 1987, like perjury to the grand jury or the Iran/Contra committees, the new guidelines will apply. And their exact purpose is to restrict the judge's flexibility. So, you will serve a jail term.

I see.

Now the discussion was over. It was after six, everyone was going home. Len Garment asked for a lift home. We could talk. He and I went back to his office, alone, and I had an almost irresistible urge to put my head on his shoulder and put my arms around him and cry. It is what I wanted to do. But I didn't. I just waited while he packed his bag, and then we left.

We talked in the car. His view was clear. Get rid of it. Put it behind you. Don't let it kill two more years. It will kill you financially. And emotionally. A plea will not. It will pass. People go through worse and come out the other side. Life goes on. Talk it over with Rachel. Call me tonight if you want.

I dropped Len off, and drove on home. I still wanted to cry, but I didn't. I could barely think. A phrase came to my mind from a movie, Marlon Brando's line from *On the Waterfront:* "I coulda been a contender." At thirty-two I had been an Assistant Secretary of State. Now here I was, driving home to tell my wife how my day had gone. I had a brief temptation to drive the car into a light pole—not to kill myself, not to hurt myself, just to give myself something else to do, to think about. It passed.

I got home and found everyone upstairs: Rachel was bathing our six-year-old, Joey. I went into the bathroom and gave him a happy smile and greeting, and a kiss. Rachel turned to me with a quizzical look, just a look, that asked everything that needed to be asked. How had it gone with Walsh? Where were we? I found that, again, I could not speak, and I simply gave her the thumbs down signal. We put the

UNDUE PROCESS

kids to bed and went downstairs and sat on the couch together, Rachel waiting for the story to be told and me feeling tons of weight, tons of sadness and regret pulling me down. I embraced her, and finally, I did cry. One long, deep sob, just one, for all that was lost, and all that was now to come.

What happened, she asked. What is it? She was one day behind in the news now, I thought, so a lifetime had passed by. Mine. I brought her up to date.

She was combative. Who's talking about pleas? They can go to hell. Let *them* plead. We'll fight this. We'll win. What is the worst thing that could happen? Prison? We would survive even that. We will survive anything. Look, she said, we know what tragedy is. Tragedy is the neighbors down the street, where the father of two girls died of brain cancer at age forty. Tragedy is Don Fortier, my friend and colleague who had been Deputy National Security adviser when he died of liver cancer at thirty-nine. This is not a tragedy. We will get through this.

That was what I needed to hear, the perfect tonic, the purest support and sustenance. I felt immeasurably better immediately, and began to joke. It all depends, I said. I knew how to get on the Elliott Abrams Diet but I'm not sure I know how to get off it. If it's 7 pounds per felony count, I'll need a whole new wardrobe. I'll have to shop in the Boys Department. I could do ads for Slim-Fast. My greatest danger now may be just plain wasting away.

Yes, Rachel said, that is probably the greatest danger. But the second greatest danger is thinking this is an unbearable tragedy. And the third greatest is giving up. Who is telling you to give up? She did not trust lawyers, the class we called "schmooze lawyers," Washington lawyers whose stock in trade was phone calls, influence peddling, power lunches. I had real lawyers, lawyer lawyers, but she was only slightly mollified. She suspected them of trying to make a deal, of being insufficiently adamant and tough, of hating Walsh less than they should. Everyone hated Walsh less than they should, we felt, except perhaps North, Poindexter, and a very few others. We felt he should be thought of and treated as roughly as one would treat Saddam Hussein. Or maybe Khaddafi.

UNDUE PROCESS

So we talked and talked, and with every passing minute I felt better, surer of myself, surer we would survive all of this, just as Rachel was saying. It is difficult to describe what happens to a husband and wife in a moment like that. I not only felt an overpowering love for her, but also a kind of physical linking, akin to the moment when the heat of a soldering iron melts two metals into liquid and they join, then harden. Each time, this bond, this marriage, became stronger, tougher, more resistant to pressure from anyone or anything outside it.

The Taxi Meter

The following day was Friday, September 27, and I met with all the lawyers again. This was my first "taxi meter day," as I called it when I told Rachel about it. No offense to them, I said, they were great, but when you sit around with four lawyers, and you are paying, when you add it all up, maybe twelve hundred dollars an hour, that's twenty dollars a minute. So when someone coughed, or spilled coffee, or when we took six minutes to order lunch, I would add it up, see the meter flipping, and smile. It costs me fifty dollars for everyone to go pee, I thought. A good cough is about a buck and a half. This amusement helped keep me sane throughout the following days, as I put a price tag on everything: pacing the room, ordering tea, sneezing. Thinking. Forgetting. I'm in the wrong line of work, I thought.

I was dead tired. I was dead tired all the time now, because I was sleeping poorly. I could not stop thinking. I could not stop having imaginary conversations with the lawyers, with Walsh, with my mother, with my brother. I could not stop making lists of whom I had to tell what, of contributors, of people who deserved advance notice of my indictment.

For indictment it was to be. That was firm. Again. If they wanted to make me a criminal, they'd have to prove it to a jury of my peers, and beyond a reasonable doubt. I was confident they had no bomb-shells, no new documents, because I knew what there was to know. Unless someone was lying, just plain lying, there was no new evi-dence. There could be no new evidence. It was my life, I knew the facts, I knew what I had known and when I learned it, and what I had told to whom. So why should I plead and do their job for them? If they wanted to make me a criminal, they'd have to do it the hard way. I felt defiant. As defiant as you can be when you aren't sleeping very well and you aren't eating very well. And you feel awful.

We were meeting in Garment's office, a big, light corner room with two walls of windows.

Should we waive the statute of limitations? Could we? Could someone check it out? Yes. You can do it. For discrete periods of time, and you can choose how long. No problem. Why should we rush? The rush is Walsh's problem, created by him and his staff; they didn't contact me for three and a half years, and now they want to rush. We should ask him to waive the statute, say for a month, and explain why.

Maybe. How much longer would this go on? I concluded that the Elliott Abrams Diet would have to presuppose statutes of limitations, or else you fade away.

Wait, said Barry Levine. They are behaving oddly. They are not behaving in a confident manner. Why don't they just send you a target letter? Why won't they say to DeVier that they are going to indict you?

And remember this: if you plead guilty, it will haunt you for a long time.

Yes, that was the problem. Not the legal or financial problem, for I thought I could deal with those. It was the moral problem. I would have given up. I would have surrendered without a fight. I would have given those bastards a victory. I would have validated their investiga-tion, their way of treating defendants. I would have let down the side, my side, the Contra side, the Reagan side, the Republican side, the tough guy–John Wayne side. How could I do that, I wondered. How could I go without a fight, always to wonder, years later, if I had done the right thing. In a year or two a trial would be over, even a short prison term would be over. Would I look back a year or two later, after copping a plea, and wonder why I had not fought for myself?

And Rachel wanted to fight. That I knew. I knew it from her words, her attitude, her expression. She was not as talented as I was at sublimating anger; she was better at feeling it well up and at letting it out, and she wanted to beat the bastards, beat them at their own game, beat them in court. They had lost the North case, would lose Poindexter too, but those were cases thrown out by higher courts. If they lost my case, before a jury, they'd have been totally discredited, ruined, smashed. How could I resist? What a contribution. Talk about not letting down the side!

Levine asked if I had ever heard of an "Alford plea." I had not. In *Alford* v. *North Carolina,* the defendant had pleaded guilty. He had told the court, if I don't plead guilty to second degree murder they'll charge me with first degree, and I might get the chair. This way, there's no chance of that. I'm not guilty at all, but this is my life, and I'm making my own decision not to risk it. The Supreme Court had accepted that as a legitimate plea, so long as it was made by an informed defendant. But trial court judges hated it; it made a mockery of "justice" when an innocent man had to plead guilty.

Would Walsh accept an *Alford* plea? someone asked. Never. For all the reasons we might want it, he would never take it. It would show the truth: that this was persecution, not prosecution, that men were forced to knuckle under by the sheer weight of the government's legal machinery. Forget it, everyone agreed; Walsh will never buy it for a second.

Levine went on. My reaction, he said, is that they still don't have their case. They don't have it. They are trying to salvage it, because they know they are in trouble. What else explains their behavior: refusing to say they'll indict, refusing to name you a target, refusing to show you any evidence. Bizarre behavior. I still believe an interview would not be in your interest, he went on. If they had powerful new evidence and wanted to convince you of its power, they'd show it to you. They'd bowl you over with it, shock you, knock you down. They would not, as they should not, ask for a decision based on their secrecy. Their failure to share any of the evidence with you is a sign of weakness on their part.

Okay, no interview. I agree. Tell them to stuff it. But wait, what if they indict me? What if it isn't a bluff? Okay, let's try them again; Pierson should go back to Walsh again. He should say, we think we know the case, and you have no case. And, I, Pierson, can't persuade Abrams to plead without any evidence. This is a critical life decision for him. Help me help him make it. You may have the right to withhold the information, but it isn't right. Don't do it. Pierson should appeal to them for help in bringing me around.

Not a bad line. It wouldn't work, though. Walsh was not a figurehead, but he was not an independent actor either; we had seen that. You could make the argument to him, but Gillen and the good old boys in the back room weren't aiming at setting standards of fairness; they wanted those pages in their scrapbooks.

We all sat in Garment's office, lawyers drifting in and out, coffee, lunch, coffee, phone calls. That taxi meter was really going. Let's see, six hours, four lawyers, Jesus Christ! Do I pay for lunch? Do I pay while they eat lunch? Only if they talk while they eat?

The atmosphere in the room was unsettling. We were all so civil, good humored, intelligent. The subjects were all aired so carefully, so thoughtfully. My own questions were admirable, serious, unemotional. I did not say, I want to kill Gillen. And Walsh. I did not say, what if I go to jail? I did not say, excuse me, I am feeling frustrated and angry, may I throw your table through the plate glass window? I did not say, do you realize my career is over? Everything I hoped and planned for, everything I wanted.

What could I do? I could not just sit there and wait for them to indict me. I could not believe they would do that, but at the same time I knew they would not pass me by. Walsh's expression had taken hold in my mind; they would not "pass it by," they needed it too much. Like a kid passing a toy store window, they wanted me too much. I was too big a prize, one of the best, one of the few left. I would not plead guilty. Not on your life. I could not sit still and let them indict me. I wanted to *act,* to save myself.

There was only one thing to do: do that interview. Sit down with

UNDUE PROCESS

them, take whatever they threw at me, answer it all, show them I wasn't afraid of them, show them I'd be dynamite on the witness stand, show them *I am innocent*. Everything Levine had said made perfect sense to me, but I could not in my gut believe it, believe that I had *no* chance of dissuading them. It was worth a try. And anyway, the downside kept shrinking. If they were going to indict, they had what they had, felt they had enough, and nothing I said would affect much.

I would do the interview. Now. Today. It was 2 P.M. Could I do it *right now?* Pierson called Walsh, who said fine, 3:30 P.M. See you soon. But wait, no, hold on, Mr. Gillen needs time, it has to be tomorrow. Tomorrow, Saturday, 10 A.M. Done.

I would go with Pierson. Pierson alone, because Walsh was still refusing to sit in the same room with Levine, Garment, and Morgan. Talk about fair play, I thought, about the right to counsel!

Still, I felt better. I was at last going to face them. Sometimes, Levine had said, prosecutors have a harder time indicting someone they've seen face to face, as a man. It was a glimmer of hope. How should I prepare? Not at all. All through law school, I had gone to the movies the night before each exam.

Into the Lion's Den

On Saturday, September 28, I met Pierson in the lobby of the building where Walsh's offices are: 555 13th Street Northwest. It's a gorgeous new building, with a huge atrium lobby, and I remembered it from my last visit, for an interview, four years before. Walsh's suite was squalid, though, and I thought the squalor had to be deliberate, a tactic adopted after there had been criticism of his spending. The waiting room was large but jammed with cartons, boxes of xerox paper, and stacked chairs, so that the space left open for "waiting" was about 8' by 10', with one guard's desk and one uncomfortable sofa.

In we went to the conference room, where a small crowd was assembled. On their side was the notetaker—an FBI agent who would testify against me if I got something wrong or changed my story—Gillen, and three other lawyers who worked for him. Walsh came in late.

We started without him, and I quickly saw what they were about. They had a wide variety of documents: memos of meetings and phone calls, State Department cables, CIA cables, personal notes of various officials. They figured they'd show me these, and I'd see the jig was up. Oh please, Mr. Gillen, Sir, I give up, I'll change my ways sir, I confess.

But what they had was trash. The first subject of discussion was a man named Felix Rodriguez, and we spent hours on him. I had testified repeatedly that I had known of him as a Bay of Pigs veteran who had gone down to El Salvador under U.S. Government auspices to help the Salvadoran air force. Their documents indicated he had also helped the private Contra arms supply network and had played a role as well in handling the legal U.S. Government humanitarian aid program that had been in effect from August 1985 to the spring of 1986, prior to the congressional decision in October 1986 to arm the Contras.

That might, if it were true, make him a key link between the Salvadoran and U.S. Governments, the official and legal U.S. Contra aid efforts, and the private supply network. But it was news to me. I had not known of any such triple role for Rodriguez, whom I had viewed as a minor figure—in fact I had no memory of ever meeting him. He had come to my attention because he had made trouble by bragging about his friendship with Vice President Bush and Bush's aide Don Gregg. I had been told that Gregg had helped place Rodriguez in El Salvador in the mid-1980s, and that Rodriguez had gone around announcing, in bars and restaurants, that he was very close to the Vice President. The conclusion people might draw was that Rodriguez represented a link between the private network and the U.S. Government—a relationship we had been trying carefully to prevent.

They showed me document after document about Rodriguez, and I repeated my denials. After about two hours of this, when Gillen asked me for the thousandth time if some new document refreshed my recollection, meaning "do you now, now at long last, admit you've been lying," I told him: "Look Mr. Gillen, you can ask me that question all day and the answer is not going to change. I have told you what I knew and what I believed. And that isn't going to change."

Okay. End of Topic One. What had I learned? That, as I had predicted, there were no secret documents affecting me. All the memos they had shown me, all the meetings they had shown me notes of, shared one curious characteristic: I had been absent from all of them.

Meetings I hadn't gone to, conversations I hadn't been part of. From this comes an indictment? I had learned one other thing, and it wasn't a surprise: they were after Don Gregg, and therefore they were after George Bush as well.

Topic Two was more familiar, and it was old, old, old. In some barren area in northern Costa Rica, the private benefactors had built an air strip. It had been used once or twice in two or three years and had had no importance at all in the Contras' efforts. But it had been an obsession of the congressional committees and had obviously become one for Walsh and his boys too. I was not nervous; I was bored. It was inconceivable that they could have anything new here, I thought, and indeed they did not.

What did I know? Who had told me? Was it North? Didn't it prove North was running the private network? Didn't you try to cover all this up, and threaten Arias—Oscar Arias Sanchez, then president of Costa Rica? Slow down. These questions were so old I hardly remembered the answers any more.

The airstrip had been part of a pattern of Contra activity that Oscar Arias had shut down after taking power. It had become inactive. There was no illicit Contra activity in Costa Rica, just some safe houses and some medical clinics.

Suddenly one day, Arias had decided his minister of public security should hold a press conference about the airstrip, discussing its construction, denouncing its existence. North had told me this and asked for my help in getting the press conference stopped. Absolutely right, I had thought at the time. Talk about gratuitous troublemaking! It was one thing for Arias to oppose U.S. policy, or to close down Contra activities in Costa Rica. He had the right to do so. But as for making common cause with the Administration's enemies on the Hill to try to change U.S. policy, as for trying to reopen what had gone before and raise questions about the government that had preceded his, that was gratuitous, and worse, it was liable to endanger people who had lawfully cooperated with the United States in previous years.

I had told Shultz about it. I had asked Ambassador Philip Habib, who liked Arias and was soon to visit him, to raise all this with him.

Those events had been examined a hundred times, but Walsh and his staff wanted to do the hundred and first. Did they have anything new? Oh yes. No documents, or testimony, to be sure. They had a theory: the State Department press guidance on this had not been forthcoming, not at all. We had not told the story. We had ignored the issue of the previous Costa Rican government's possible role and had not said anything about the private Contra supply network. The guidance had been bland, uninformative; it had been misleading.

That was true. Bland, uninformative, even misleading. Not all press guidances in the Department are like that—maybe only half are. I was amazed. How far did these guys plan to go? If they didn't like something Reagan or Shultz had said at a press conference, were they planning to indict him? They didn't like a press guidance that ninety-seven people had cleared, and they wanted an indictment? Did they plan to go after every press officer in the government from now on? Could press secretaries qualify for combat pay?

Walsh was silent, and Gillen did all the talking. I asked Gillen whether press guidances, and efforts to criminalize what was in them, didn't raise a First Amendment issue. He didn't bite. Walsh, who hadn't said a word, not a word all day, remained silent. Okay, I thought, First Amendment gone. Their efforts to stop me from bringing the counsel of my choice in with me had violated the Sixth Amendment. Two down, eight to go.

Now, on to North. Surely I had known what he'd been doing. Everything he'd been doing. Surely I had known he was more than a messenger, a contact, with the private network, that he was its Chief Executive Officer. Nope. I had not. I had told them that four years before, as I'd told the Tower Commission, the Iran/Contra committees, and anyone else who'd asked. What was new? Documents? Interviews? Evidence? No. None that they showed me. There was an implication, a whiff in the air, that Fiers or North might say otherwise. Had said otherwise. It didn't surprise me. I had no idea what North would say, and he had already testified to the Congress that everyone knew everything. Fiers was awaiting sentencing, and maybe he was being cooperative, even more cooperative than the facts would allow. Maybe they were "helping" him remember things that had never happened. And maybe it was all a bluff. Maybe North and Fiers were not cooperating with them, maybe the record stood as I knew it, and these guys had nothing, *nothing,* incriminating me.

Their questions suggested this. They were caricature questions, Perry Mason questions. What happened at the meeting on September 25, 1986? What did North say to you on March 8, 1986? What did he say on December 10, 1985? Who attended the meeting on April 3? I could hardly believe they were asking me all this seriously. We had now spent an entire day, from 10 A.M. to 6 P.M., in that little room, going through gigantic piles of documents. And what did they have? At bottom, just what they had had four or five years before. For this they had spent fifty million dollars?

At the end, when all their questions were asked, I said I wanted to say something. What I *wanted* to say, really, was, You miserable, filthy bastards, you bloodsuckers! You, Gillen, trying to build a career over my bleeding body, and Alan Fiers's as well, trying to make up for losing the North case without the slightest care about the people you maim in the process. You, Walsh, eighty years old and nothing else to do but stay in this job till the grim reaper gets you. Is this your idea of America? The entire weight of the government, with prosecutors, investigators, the FBI, goes to bankrupt and to smear a few former officials because the President's policies were too hot for the Democratic Congress to handle? Is that what America is all about? Coming at me five years later, when everyone's memory is failing, to pick up a detail here and a phone call there and try to ruin my life? That's what you want America to be?

That's what I wanted to say. It boiled up inside me, it had kept me awake the night before, made me unable to think sometimes because the desire to say it was so powerful.

But self-interest is equally powerful, more powerful, so I said something different.

I said, Look, I spent my time in the government doing my job, following the President's and Secretary's instructions. I did not feather my nest. I spent zero time, zero, setting up future clients, meeting with bankers, investors, future employers, because I thought that was not right. Trying to follow the policy was my job. Then came this scandal, and I had been paying and paying and paying. For five years. The pressures on my family had been enormous. The toll was great, I said. I had meant to give them examples, but when it came to it, I did not. The time the ''Witness for Peace'' people demonstrated at my house, screaming out epithets and calling me a baby killer while my kids, virtual prisoners in the house, peeked out the windows. The times people accosted me in a restaurant or airport to denounce me, with my family standing right there. The clients who had said, we'd like to work with you, but it's just a bit too controversial for us. And now, five years later, when my life had just returned to normal, here they were. And it wasn't enough to harass me, it wasn't enough to denounce me, as they could, in their report; they had to go further. They had to brand me a criminal. They could not be satisfied, they would not be doing their jobs, unless they had done that? And I asked Walsh not to do it. And there was dead silence in the room, until he replied, ''I understand.'' And the ''interview'' was over.

I felt great. I felt victorious. They had not shaken me. I had made my speech, maybe not the one I had made inside my head in bed late at night, but a good one. I had walked into the lion's den and out again. I had answered every question. I was exhausted but not at all tired, because I was on a high. I was a winner. I had done something. I was better than they were. Maybe there was a happy ending to all this. How could they indict me now? How could they hope to win this case? It was ludicrous. They had *no* evidence that I had known of any illegal acts, any Boland Amendment violations, any role by North that went beyond communicating with the private network. They couldn't indict me. They just couldn't. And if they did, fine. Let 'em. We'd kill 'em. That would be a real contribution I could make: destroy Walsh's reputation, beat him and his boys, show that their whole operation was a disgrace.

I had finally met the great Walsh, and Gillen, and all the boys. I had not been not overly impressed. Walsh, rail-thin in his three-piece suit, had tried to appear sober but benign, friendly in his stiff, judge-like way. It occurred to me how much he looked like a Lawrence Walsh puppet a kid might make. He had said very little, and the energy in the room, on that side of the room, had come from Gillen. Assistant U.S. Attorney from Atlanta. Career prosecutor. Pleasant looking, I

had been told; killer with a choirboy face. I had found him very
unpleasant, and I knew why. What he had communicated was a very
sure sense that I was a liar, a criminal, hiding facts, misleading him
and the Judge, not coming clean. He had exuded a sense of self-
righteousness I found insufferable. He believed, he truly believed, he
was doing God's work here, exposing the vast criminal conspiracy that
unenlightened folk called the Reagan Administration. I had been in it,
of it, enthusiastic about it, so I was a part of that conspiracy. He was
just pinning down the details. Another Calvinist, I thought. Maybe all
prosecutors are, maybe they all come to believe they have been Chosen
to Punish Sin. And these guys in Walsh's office accused the Reaganites
of being zealots!

I was shocked by one facet of that day. Here we had all sat, a
bunch of guys, all lawyers, and we had talked, argued, debated. And
when we were finished, I would go home, and they would decide
whether and how they were going to wreak havoc on my life. Who
gave them this power? To whom did they report? What were the
regulations, the standards? They sat there, invincible in their smug-
ness, they listened to no one, reported to no one, followed no rules.
Everything was new. They did what they wanted. Now *that* was power.
Fifty years ago Robert Jackson, then Attorney General and soon to go
on the Supreme Court, had said that "the prosecutor has more control
over life, liberty, and reputation than any other person in America." I
was learning what he meant.

But that was a philosophical problem. That was an issue for some
magazine article. In the concrete what I had seen was that they were
just guys, nasty guys with power, but just guys, and that they had no
evidence. There was no secret memo, no transcript, nothing new.

Rachel and I celebrated. We could see freedom just around the
corner.

But I had spent the entire day away from home. What could I tell
the children? It would have been obvious, even to children less intelligent, that something was up, and that it was bad. Now I had lost an
entire Saturday, a day when I would normally have gone to synagogue
with my oldest boy, had lunch with the kids at home, and then done
some combination of shopping, playing ball, napping, reading, and

taking them to friends' houses, and probably would have ended up taking everyone out to dinner. Not today—so what was up? We had to tell them something.

This was one reason, one powerful, powerful reason, not to plead guilty. How the hell, I had wondered, do you explain copping a plea to a kid? How do you explain saying, Yes, I committed a crime. But I didn't have to face that. This, fighting off an indictment, was much easier.

Look, I said to the kids, when I was in the State Department I knew a lot of secrets. Lots and lots, and I wasn't allowed to tell anyone. You remember Nicaragua, and the Contras, and how they were fighting the Communists in Nicaragua? Well, I knew lots of secrets about that, and Secretary Shultz and President Reagan didn't want me to tell. Now, some people are saying, you should have told Congress. You had to tell. When they asked you, you had to tell, and not telling is a crime. And I am saying, no it isn't. So we may have a court case, where they accuse me, they say I did something wrong, and I say, No, I didn't. And it might take a year. And if it happens, there will be lots of TV cameras around for a day or so. But then, life will be pretty normal, and you don't have to worry about it. Instead of going to my office, to write my book, I'll go to court. But for you, for us, life will really be the same after the first day or two.

They thought about this. Joey, who was six, took it in, but he asked no questions. Sarah, nine, wondered if she'd be on TV. Then she asked, how can it be wrong to keep secrets? Wasn't that part of your job, Daddy? And if you gave Congress the secrets, would they have kept them? Wouldn't they have told?

Well, I figured, she understands it fine. She understands it better than Lawrence Walsh, and he's eighty. She's nine. Rachel jumped in to say, Daddy was supposed to keep secrets, but you're not. If a grownup asks you to keep a secret, or hurts you, or says something bad to you, or embarrasses you, and says keep it a secret, you don't. You tell your mom and dad. Sure, Sarah said; I know. It was Daddy's job to keep secrets, and it's my job to tell them to my parents. Punto final! as the Latins say.

Jacob, ten, listened carefully to a slightly more sophisticated version of the facts, and then asked some questions. If they are accusing *you*, he said, what about Ronald Reagan? What about George Bush? Why don't they get accused too?

Sarah understood it better than Walsh; Jacob understood it better than I did. Why indeed? I left Rachel to try and answer questions that I had tried hard not to ask myself.

SUNDAY, SEPTEMBER 29

The Interview: Rodriguez, Hasenfus, and the Sultan of Brunei

On Sunday morning, I set up a conference call with all the lawyers. Pierson briefed the others on what had happened and gave his general impressions.

They sure want something on Felix Rodriguez, Pierson said. If Elliott could give them something linking Rodriguez, and knowledge of his activities, to Bush or to Don Gregg, they'd buy it fast. I understood that; if I could incriminate someone, someone higher up than me, I might get off the hook. That's the system of justice, I told myself again.

But, said Pierson, there's some danger here. Elliott told them, as he had told others in past years, that he had never met Rodriguez. One count of the Clair George indictment states that George lied when he said he had never met Secord. That was much easier to prove than some complicated argument about what you thought or didn't think in 1986. If they can show Elliott met with Rodriguez, that's a problem. They also have him saying he knew very, very little about Rodriguez's work with the private network and even with the U.S. humanitarian aid program. If they think they can show he did have that knowledge, that's a sure count in the indictment. That's okay, I thought; it wasn't true, so they can't show it.

Pierson went on, I'd sure love to know what other people are telling them about what State knew, and Elliott knew. But they don't appear to have the goods. There are lots of notes, transcripts, meeting memos about Rodriguez and his role, and Elliott is conspicuously absent in them. They don't have the goods when it comes to Rodriguez, so that does not help them show Elliott knew of any U.S. Government ties to the private network, or of any illegal activity.

Now, about that airstrip in Costa Rica. They sure spent a lot of time on it. The question is, what is the punch line? The real core of it seems to be their view that Elliott knew it had been set up with U.S. Government help—illegal help to the private network—and his efforts to stop the Arias press conference about it were his part in the cover-up.

They feel the same way about that State Department press guidance: more cover-up. Now, they asked Elliott why the press guidance had not been more accurate, or more forthcoming, and he told them the answer was politics. The congressional vote on the full $100 million in U.S. Government support for the Contras was then just weeks away, and he said he didn't want to give the Administration's political enemies any ammunition. They'd have used it against the Administration, and maybe it would have turned a close vote around and defeated the program. Now, they can try to construct a Section 1001 charge on that. They can say the press guidance was really a false statement to Congress, a false statement meant to influence and mislead the Congress, the functional equivalent of false testimony.

One thousand and one. Those numbers I had come to know well. False Testimony to Congress. Not perjury; that was a different law, and of course you had to be under oath for perjury. Section 1001 was for unsworn statements. And Walsh was applying it not to theft, not to financial peculation, but to *testimony*. I still couldn't believe it: for the first time in American history, a prosecutor was saying, we don't like the way you testified on *policy* matters, so we are going to call it a crime. This was Lawrence Walsh's contribution to our freedom, to the great saga of American democracy. Don't like your testimony, don't like your policy—BANG!, off to jail.

UNDUE PROCESS

Congressmen and Senators could say what they wanted, of course; the Constitution plainly said that anything a member said on the floor was protected by the "Speech and Debate Clause" of Article I. That was a carryover from the efforts of Parliament to protect itself from the Tudor and Stuart kings and their abuse of the law courts to pressure Parliamentarians.

Peter Morgan had written a brilliant law review article about all this, and I had read it. Everyone had always perceived the latitude for Executive Branch officials to be, if not equally broad, then extremely broad anyway. Otherwise you would upset the balance of powers between the branches, and Cabinet and White House officials and their assistants could be hauled up in court on any controversial issue. Presidents and their men had deliberately misled Congress any number of times. Recently, for example, Kennedy and his advisers had done so on the Cuban Missile crisis; Johnson and McNamara had done so on Vietnam. Roosevelt on the start of World War II. What had Carter withheld on human rights and political conditions, the gun-running, and the narcotics trafficking in Panama to get the Canal Treaties passed? No one would ever know. That was politics.

But not any more. Not with Judge Walsh on the case. Now they would take your testimony, your answers to questions—not planned and written documents carefully drawn up and reviewed, but your spur-of-the-moment answer to someone's question—and they would go over it five years later, and if they didn't like it, BOOM! Get yourself a lawyer. See the grand jury. What did you say to Ollie North on November 10, 1985? Go directly to jail, do not pass Go, pay one million dollars.

So they didn't like my press guidance of September 6, 1986. They might charge a 1001 violation, Pierson said, or they might charge obstruction of justice. Trying to obfuscate, so a congressional investigation would fail. Something like that. I sat in my kitchen and wondered, where is Eugene Ionesco when you need him?

Next we get to Hasenfus, Pierson went on. Eugene Hasenfus had been a ne'er-do-well "kicker," a man who kicks cargo out the door of a cargo plane. He had done it in Vietnam, where he had worked indirectly for the CIA in the 1970s, and much later, in 1986, in Nicaragua. The private network had hired a bunch of men with Southeast

Asian experience, and three of them had taken off on October 4, 1986, from El Salvador to make a drop to Contra troops inside Nicaragua. They had been shot down, and the other two had been killed in the crash. Hasenfus had survived. He had been captured by the Sandinistas and jailed in Managua. The Sandinistas had immediately claimed the plane was sent by the U.S. Government, that the whole private network had been supported and directed by Washington.

I had been the principal spokesman for the Reagan Administration on this issue. I had appeared on radio and TV and in the press saying publicly what I had told Shultz privately: there was no U.S. Government involvement in that flight. None. Period. Sure, we had thought this private network was great, and we had urged people generally to help out. Reagan himself had met with people doing so and had given them pep talks. So had I. And I had known that North was the point of contact with them, knew who some of them were, could send messages back and forth to and from them. But this had not been our flight, and this had not been our network. Speaking in early October 1986, I had been absolutely confident of that.

I had been wrong or, as I later put it in my testimony to the Iran/Contra committees, "completely honest and completely wrong." That state of grace had lasted only two weeks, for on October 23, 1986, my CIA counterpart, Fiers's boss, had told me there was something going on. The CIA's station chief in Costa Rica had somehow been involved in the flights, in the private network. I had immediately gone to Shultz with this information, told him what I had been told, and railed against the Agency. I had been out there for two weeks, I told Shultz, saying there were no U.S. Government connections, and now it seemed there were. The spooks were screwing it all up.

But Walsh and his boys did not believe any of this. They did not believe that until October 23, until the CIA revealed to me that there had been a CIA role, I had not known there was a U.S. Government role in the operation. They have no new information on this, Pierson said, but if they indict, this is clearly going to be a count. They may say Elliott knew North was involved, or they may say he knew Rodriguez was involved, but either way they will do both a 1001 count and an obstruction count. They can't prove what was in Elliott's head when

UNDUE PROCESS

he testified in October 1986, but they'll say his categorical statements were meant to mislead Congress and obstruct their investigation.

And they'll go back to "Monitor Ollie," too, Pierson said. In an early meeting with Shultz, soon after being appointed to run the Latin America bureau, I had told Shultz I didn't know much about North's activities or about the private network. He had told me to find out some more, and I had written in my notebook, "Monitor Ollie." I remembered that phrase well. I had written it in my notebook in September 1985 and had not seen it again until the notebook was demanded by the Iran/Contra committees as evidence for their hearing—along with my telephone log and a million memos to and from me.

Looking through that little notebook, I had come across the phrase and immediately understood that the investigators would love it. And ask about it, and ask about it. And they had, as had all the congressmen after them. Mr. Abrams, did you monitor Ollie? How did you monitor Ollie? When did you monitor Ollie? Why didn't you monitor Ollie? I had seen it all coming, sitting there at my kitchen table, and all I had to do was tear that one looseleaf page out and throw it away. Gone. No questions asked. But I had not done it. Destroying evidence is a real crime, I had thought, and no matter how much you hate the investigators and the congressmen who will grandstand this, and this whole goddam circus, don't do it.

As I listened to Pierson now, five years later, I was not sure what I would do if I had to do it over again. One thing was certain: no more notes. No more notebooks. That lesson I had learned.

In the late 1980s I spoke to a group of college students who were summer interns in Washington. What advice do you have for us, they asked, as we start a career here in Washington? God only knows what high-toned philosophy they were expecting, but my answer was low and direct: "Do not buy a notebook. Don't take notes. Don't write anything down." Notes are things people will use against you five years later when no one, not even you, can remember exactly what they meant. Notes are small time bombs you set for yourself, at least with guys like Walsh walking around they are. "Did you monitor Ollie on October 4? On October 5? It's only five years ago, come on, it's *your* notebook." Yes, and it's the last one I will ever have.

Pierson continued. They will say, Shultz told Elliott to find out where the arms and money for the private network are coming from, and he deliberately did not, he tried very hard *not* to find out, to avoid knowledge. He didn't want to ask the right questions.

And, he added, as I listened to all of this yesterday my thought was they could show Elliott's October 1986 statements were perhaps reckless, given the state of his knowledge, but they could not show any actual knowledge of their falsity. Is recklessness actionable under the criminal statutes in question? Whew, I thought, relieved at Pierson's question. Of course not. You had to have guilty knowledge, right? Wrong, Morgan said. There are cases saying that "conscious avoidance" of knowledge, or "willful blindness," won't get you off the hook; there is such a thing as constructive knowledge. This is a dangerous area, Morgan said; the "should have known" argument will be a tough one.

Finally, Pierson said, they got to fundraising.

Another old chestnut. Congress had approved $27 million in humanitarian aid for the Contras in the summer of 1985, meant to last until the full $100 million program would be voted in March 1986. The only trouble was, we had lost the March vote in the House. It had been very close, and we had retained some confidence that we'd win it sooner or later, but who could say when that would be? Tip O'Neill was adamantly opposed and was pulling out all the stops. He was taking advice on Central America from a niece of his who was a Maryknoll nun, and she apparently believed the Sandinistas were distributing loaves and fishes, bible in hand. And meanwhile, as the spring of 1986 wore on, the Contras' situation was getting desperate. They were running out of food, out of medicine. Something had to be done.

Reagan had called his senior advisers to the White House Situation Room in May 1986 to figure it out, and everyone had agreed on seeing if some foreign government might put in some money. No one at that meeting mentioned that there was a precedent: the Saudis were kicking in two million a month already. No one mentioned it to me, and when, a few months later, Secretary Shultz had found out, he had not mentioned it to me either. No one had ever told me.

UNDUE PROCESS

But once it had been agreed that we should try, "we" had turned out to be "I." I had been instructed by the Secretary to come up with some ideas, but no dictatorships (bad image for the Contras), and no country that depended on U.S. aid (because it would look too much as if we were muscling them). As I had pondered it, trying to think of who had money to burn, I had realized we needed some oil producer, but not an Arab tyranny. Which had left us with Venezuela and Brunei. As I knew the president of Venezuela, for Venezuela was on my turf, and thought he would not do this, that had left us with Brunei. So Brunei it had been, an obscure sultanate in Southeast Asia whose ruler was arguably the world's richest man. How much were we to ask for? Well, that $27 million in humanitarian aid had been supposed to last for nine months, which meant three million a month, and we had needed three months or so to tide us over until we could win a vote on the Hill, which meant nine million. So I had rounded it off: ten million.

Shultz had said okay, good idea, and in fact he was going to visit Brunei as part of an Asia trip pretty soon. During his visit he had raised the subject generally with the Sultan but had not made the pitch; that had been left for me to do, in August 1986, when the Sultan had happened to be visiting London.

It had all been arranged with great secrecy through the State Department and the U.S. Embassy in Brunei. I had traveled to London, using my own passport, and registered at the Hilton in my own name. I had called the Sultan's suite at the Dorchester and asked for the aide I was supposed to meet with, using a code name we had agreed upon so he would know who was calling, but the British—whom he assumed were monitoring his phones—would not. We had met in the lobby, had taken a walk in Hyde Park, and I had made the pitch. Ten million. The Contras needed it, the Sultan wouldn't miss it, so why not?

Why not indeed? Word had come a few weeks later, from Brunei's capital of Bandar Seri Begawan, that the Sultan had said yes. A done deal. Except the money had never arrived. Later on, we had found out why: Oliver North had provided the account number, and his secretary, Fawn Hall, had transposed two digits in typing it out for me. The Sultan's money had gone into the wrong Swiss bank account, from which it had later been recovered after the Iran/Contra scandal blossomed. I never found out if the Sultan was mad at the United States, or mad at me; I had, in a certain sense, saved him ten million dollars, and later, whenever I found myself short of money, I would wonder what he had done with "my" ten million bucks.

But what all this had meant in the fall of 1986 was that when the Hasenfus plane was shot down, we had as yet received not a dime from the Sultan. And as I had known nothing about the Saudi money, I had been absolutely confident I could say that whatever the Contras were living on, it wasn't foreign government money. When the Congress had held hearings in the aftermath of the Hasenfus shoot-down, that is just what I had told them.

Walsh and his staff didn't like it. You knew money was coming, they told me; you knew it was pledged. How could you say there was no foreign money? Simple, I replied. There was no foreign money. I knew what was being implied by those Congressional queries about foreign funding: that money from the Hill was not needed because foreign governments were paying for this; or, that there had been plenty of money but the Contra leaders had stolen it all.

Walsh and his boys put a sinister interpretation on all this. Their theory was that, with the congressional vote on the $100 million just days away, I had not wanted Congress snooping around asking who had given, or pledged, what. I had testified for the first time after the Hasenfus shoot-down on October 10; the conference report approving the $100 million for the Contras came to the floor on October 17.

Listening to Pierson now, I had two reactions. First, the President, on behalf of the United States and acting through the Secretary of State and an Assistant Secretary, had asked a foreign ruler for help. He had replied, can you pledge confidentiality? And we had all officially said yes. Shultz had told me, do not tell anyone about this, this is a secret we must keep. I had kept it. The Department had gone to extraordinary lengths to protect the cables regarding this matter, and it had not leaked. When I testified, I had said nothing about it, and that was not so hard, for the money hadn't arrived. *We had no foreign government money of which I was aware.* And now they were saying that it was a crime.

UNDUE PROCESS

They called it a crime not to have told Congress that the Sultan had said, yes, he would send the money, even though as far as we knew he had not sent it, even though we had begun to wonder if he ever would. It would all have leaked from Congress in five minutes flat. I could tell Walsh of times when Congressional staffers had run out of a closed, secret committee meeting directly to the telephones to call reporters. That was no crime, that was of no interest to him. But when I had kept the word of the United States, now that was a crime.

And second, I began to see that Barry Levine had been right. He had always opposed the interview, and now I saw why. I had done very well, but still I had damaged myself. I had given Walsh one key item: *motive*. You didn't tell about the Brunei money for the same reason you misled Congress about the Hasenfus flight and official ties to the private network, Mr. Abrams. You admitted it to us yourself. You said yourself you were worried about that vote just a few days down the road, worried your political opponents would use anything you said against you and against the program. So you just shut up.

Now Pierson summed up. We saw a lot of paper, he said. While their case on all counts is circumstantial, they have a lot to present. It is not flimsy, and it does not consist of things North or Fiers or others may or may not have said to them. Still, he said, my overall impression of how the day went is that Elliott did not hurt himself. If he did, it's because we'll have that FBI 302 report with lots and lots of "I don't remember." If Elliott has a new memory at the trial, that will be a problem. Overall in terms of their attitude toward Elliott, he helped himself. They'll be more sympathetic or at least perplexed as to his statements on Felix Rodriguez, because they realize they have no direct evidence and Elliott is so very firm in his denials. They do not have a lot of sympathy with the statements, those categorical statements, he made after the Hasenfus shoot-down. They believe he should not have done that, although he did pretty well in explaining his views at the time, his thinking at that moment. Still, they find all that pretty hard to swallow. They didn't spend too much time on fundraising and Brunei, but that may just mean it is what it is, the testimony is there, no point in going over it again and again.

And, Elliott gave a powerful statement at the end, telling them of the effect this had already had on his life. Pierson repeated a story I had told Walsh and company. Once in early 1982 when I was Assistant Secretary of State for Human Rights, I had testified with the then Assistant Secretary for Inter-American Affairs, Tom Enders, about the guerrilla war in El Salvador and U.S. aid to that country. You know, I had said to Enders, I'm happy to testify, glad to do it, but why are you and I doing it? Why isn't the Under Secretary, or the Deputy Secretary, or the Secretary testifying? Enders had turned to me with a grim smile and replied ''Because it's a dirty little war and they don't want to touch it.''

Walsh took the point, Pierson said. When the two of them chatted briefly after my interview, Walsh had said that nothing bothered him more in his job than the fact that those at the most senior levels of government were escaping their responsibilities, while those on the firing line, like Elliott, did not escape, and were indeed the very targets he was ending up concentrating on.

Jesus Christ, I thought, don't give me your tortured soul routine, don't ask us all for our sympathy, don't tell me ''this hurts me more than it hurts you.'' Don't do it! Drop it. Go home. Drop dead. Do something useful.

And one more thing, Pierson said. Walsh had ended their chat by raising, again, that old issue of a proffer. Oh yes, the proffer. The perfect out for Walsh. He could salve his terribly guilt-ridden conscience, and make Gillen happy, if only he could get me to rat on someone. Hand us Gregg, or Shultz, or someone appetizing. Then you might be off the hook. Justice in America, I thought. Anyway, Pierson had told Walsh the truth: Elliott has no information on anyone. He has nothing to tell you.

Now what? Well, Walsh had said his staff would do a ''careful review'' in-house of all that I had said. And Pierson, who had a trial in Oklahoma now, would return late Wednesday night and see Walsh Thursday at 10:30 A.M. Don't misread what Walsh said to me, Pierson warned; he isn't pulling away from that misdemeanor count. It could be he wants to think about how ''minimal'' he might make it, to use his word. The only thing they would clearly be receptive to today would be a proffer. You should continue to think about that, and not only about things you know, but also about where they might look, how they might think about things, whom they might talk to.

This was revolting, but Pierson was doing his job: he was trying to get me off. Walsh was clearly desperate for a proffer, and would pay for it in the currency available to him. Which was my future.

Tell him to drop dead, I thought, with his proffers and his "something minimal" and his "disposition." I will fight this. No way will he get me to compromise.

We agreed to meet, all of us, before Pierson saw Walsh again. We would meet on Thursday at 8 A.M. at Garment's office. Meanwhile, we would try to pull together all the information we could. If lawyers for others whom Walsh was pursuing would talk to us, we would find out what they knew and what their clients were saying to Walsh about me.

And we had some legal research to do, too. Could that press guidance really be covered by an obstruction charge? Had such a thing ever been done before? What about that "willful blindness" issue? What about the issue of "recantation"? Under the perjury statute, you were off the hook if you recanted soon after the perjury. There was no such clause in the 1001 false testimony statute, but some courts had read it in: how could the defense of recantation be available for the worse crime, perjury, but not the lesser offense of false testimony? This might matter, for I had testified in the Senate Intelligence Committee on November 25, 1986, and had not mentioned the solicitation of Brunei, and then I had asked Shultz for permission to reveal it and had done so ten days later.

One more thing: Sofaer, now back in Washington, was seeing Walsh the next day, Monday. He was a friendly voice, a former judge like Walsh, and maybe he could persuade Walsh that actual criminal prosecution just wasn't called for here. At the very least, he might be able to tell us what he thought my chances of escaping indictment were.

So Pierson left for Oklahoma, to return in four days. And I had a normal Sunday. "Normal." That meant calling my mother to tell her what was up, then telling my in-laws, then telling my brother, then a few conversations with my lawyers. Hour after hour on the phone, until my ear hurt. I thought of buying one of those headsets operators wear. Maybe they have a special model for defendants, I told myself. Or maybe a special discount for victims of the Special Prosecutor.

The day before, Saturday, a friend had sent me in the mail a statement from Justice Jackson, made in 1940 when he was still Attorney General of the United States:

> With the law books filled with a great assortment of crimes, a prosecutor stands a fair chance of finding at least a technical violation of some act on the part of almost anyone . . . it is not a question of discovering the commission of a crime . . . it is a question of picking the man and then . . . pin[ning] some offense on him. It is in this realm . . . that the greatest danger of abuse of prosecuting power lies. It is here that law enforcement becomes personal.

I thought of faxing that over to Gillen. I thought of sending him Terry Eastland's wonderful book, *Ethics, Politics, and the Independent Counsel* (Washington: 1989), and underlining the sentence that reads, "The traditional assumption in law enforcement is not that every criminal infraction should be prosecuted, or even that every criminal allegation should be investigated." They wanted me to proffer George Bush and George Shultz. I had in mind Justice Jackson and Terry Eastland.

MONDAY, SEPTEMBER 30

Family Matters

Until Pierson returned to Washington, action would now slow down.

I spoke to Sofaer after he saw Walsh. He was guarded. He was my friend, but he was Walsh's as well, and he would keep a confidence. He confirmed what I had felt: the meeting Saturday had gone well for me. I had made a good impression on them. However, the situation remained very serious. They were not going to walk away from this. Sofaer had given them the correct impression about my mindset: I would fight any criminal outcome. He had himself urged some noncriminal way out: could not someone devise a civil penalty? In some securities or antitrust cases, defendants pay civil fines or sign consent decrees, or the agency issues cease and desist orders, or gets an injunction. Something along those lines was not foreclosed, Sofaer felt. That kind of scenario seemed to him alive, and he was for that, but he wanted to impress upon me the seriousness of the situation.

Now, could I believe what Walsh had said to Sofaer? They knew he would be speaking to me, or probably guessed it. Maybe they had decided to do nothing but were using Sofaer to try to scare me into folding. It was possible. When Sofaer told them I'd fight a criminal outcome, maybe they didn't believe him. Maybe they thought that he had that impression because I wanted him to have it, and to convey it to them. Walsh was "not the village idiot," one of my lawyers had said to me; he would wonder whether we were trying to "use" Sofaer. Just as I wondered if they were. Nice, I thought; Abe volunteers to help, pure altruism, and everyone involved is now parsing his every sentence and assuming the other side is using him to float misleading messages.

I now had three days to think, anyway. How much time could you spend thinking in seventy-two hours? The whole seventy-two hours? No, for several reasons. First, the children. It was a cardinal principle to try to put them first, to try to make their lives seem as normal as possible. Normal breakfast times, getting ready for school; normal evenings, with dinner, baths, stories. Then I had a few meetings scheduled that week, and I decided to go to them. One was a small luncheon with the Romanian foreign minister, who was visiting Washington. And I had to see one client on Tuesday. It became a game for me: how cheerful could I be? How relaxed, insouciant, calm, could I be, so that if things turned out badly, if I were indicted in a week, people would later say, "My God! I saw him last week and he was cool as a cucumber!"?

During the week I reviewed the bidding. My brother was worried about fighting this to the end, and he wondered how smart I was to write off a plea bargain as a possibility. How can you raise a million dollars? he asked. How long will a trial take? Juries being what they are, you might lose at trial; is it worth the risk? Why don't you put it behind you, just get it over with? This single-count misdemeanor that no one ever heard of, it isn't even false testimony, you won't get disbarred; think about it. This argument pissed me off. He should be saying, Fight! Here's some money, don't let the slimeballs do it to you, this is still America, Fight! He wasn't. And his arguments were good ones; that was the worst part.

My answers were better, I thought. I'd be a criminal; think about it, a *criminal*. You say, get on with your future; what future? As a criminal? A trial would be over in a year or two, and I can live through it, and after it's over and I'm exonerated I'll be very glad I didn't plead and make myself a criminal. If they think I am, let them prove it; I won't help them get there. I don't need a million bucks, really, just a few hundred thousand, maybe half a million. The lawyers don't always get paid.

I thought, why did I ever start this? My father had been an immigration lawyer. The big Wall Street firms had always sneered at that kind of law; most people in it were solo practitioners or in firms of two or three people, as my father had been. You never made a big fortune, mostly because your clients were usually poor, or at best middle class, and they could not afford the fees the big firms charged corporations. And those clients were not the well-clad, well-spoken executives who came to see corporate lawyers. They were uneducated, poor, badly dressed. They were mechanics or cooks, or maids.

But it was great practice, a wonderful practice, whatever the pompous stiffs on Wall Street thought, because your clients were people, real people, and you could help them. You helped them by getting them visas to America, or by getting them permission to stay in America as permanent residents, or by getting them, in the end, citizenship. You made people Americans. You changed their lives, and this was not a matter of politics or psychology, it was no abstraction. You made people Americans and you changed their lives.

I still met old clients of my father. Guys who had come here as kids, twenty years old, who were now forty or fifty, had three children, and owned a gas station or two, or had become their company's vice president, or had made a million bucks. And they would tell me, God bless your father. He made this all possible. And they would cry, and so would I.

My brother had gotten out of Yale Law School and said no to the Wall Street firms, and joined my father, and they had called the firm Abrams & Abrams. I had worked there during the summers when I was in law school, but upon graduating from Harvard in 1973 I had decided the world was too big, too exciting. I wanted something else. So I had said no, this is not for me, and had gone to Wall Street. Which turned out not to be for me. And by March of 1975 I had made my way to Washington.

U N D U E   P R O C E S S

Six years later I was an Assistant Secretary of State. My father had come to my swearing in, in March 1981, and he could not possibly have been prouder or happier. On December 10, 1981, I had brought my parents into the Oval Office to meet the President. Exactly four weeks later, before they had even developed the official photos, my father had died, at sixty-seven, of heart disease. And nine years after that, fifteen years after arriving in Washington, I was about to be indicted.

So I listened to my brother talk, and I wondered. Would I be happier today if I had just gone to Abrams & Abrams? If you had told me then that in going to Washington I'd end up indicted, I'd have thought you were crazy. And what's more, you would have *been* crazy. Anyway, I told myself, stop thinking about what you should have done or might have done. It gets you nowhere. And it hurts too much. I found myself wondering, if my father were alive, could he have stood the pain of this? To see this happen to me? I had missed him every day, every day, since his death, and now I said to myself, are you glad he isn't here because you would be giving him too much pain?

The question took my breath away. I was sitting on the sofa, at home, and I froze. I thought, I am glad he is not feeling this pain, but I miss him so much, especially right now. And then I thought, but I would not be the one causing him pain. *They* would be. The guys who are doing this to me. And because of the pain they would be causing him if he were alive, I hated them even more.

My father had not been a Lawrence Walsh kind of lawyer. Walsh had been senior partner of Davis, Polk & Wardwell, one of Wall Street's most prestigious firms. The kind of place that, when my father was in law school, had had no Jews. The kind of place that probably hadn't handled immigration matters during Walsh's tenure, because they were "declassé," they were the bailiwick of Jews and Italians in midtown.

Walsh had been a neutron bomb kind of lawyer: the neutron bomb that kept the buildings, the factories, and the bridges intact, and only killed the people in them. The true corporate lawyer, who worried only about keeping the corporation, the stock, and the factory intact; and wasn't that, I asked myself, just what I was seeing now reflected in his new role as Independent Counsel? He didn't give a goddamn about people, about families, whatever his occasional crocodile tears. He would tell you he was defending the institutions, or the Constitution, or something like that, and the mere people he ran up against could not be permitted to get in the way. Crunch!

Later I heard they had actually fingerprinted Ollie North's wife, and taken her mug shot, to give him just a whiff of terror about what might happen to his children; but I guess that must have been in the interest of justice, I guess the Constitution must have required it.

Just as it apparently required them to try to wreck my career and brand me a criminal, and say no to every alternative and every argument and every plea we put forward. Yes, of course, quite clear: how can democracy survive if we let Elliott Abrams go free?

If worse came to worst, I would be sent to prison. It happened to people, I knew that. I never, never mentioned that possibility, or allowed it to be mentioned, in the presence of my mother or the children. The children would be terrified by the thought, and it seemed a crazy thought. Anyway, if we ever came to that it would be years away, so it was a non-thought. It was not allowed to exist. With my mother, it was simply a way to avoid needless suffering. She was smart, she knew what was at stake here, and she had my brother to answer any questions she had. There was no reason to make it worse than it was. I had slowly, artfully I hoped, introduced the whole problem, increased the sense of risk each day, opened the door to indictment as a possibility, in the least shocking, least painful way possible. It seemed to have worked.

My mother, however, was with my brother on the plea question. Don't go through another year of it, or two years or more. Get it over with. Let them call whatever they want to call you, but get it behind you. Think what two years of this, and a debt of a million dollars, will do to you, your family, the children. Is it worth it? For what? My brother had pointed out that no one even remembered who won these cases. People remembered someone had been indicted, there had been a scandal, there had been a trial. The verdict came a year or two later, and who could really remember which of the Watergate people was convicted? How many people remembered that Ray Donovan had been totally exonerated? Had John Connally won or lost?

I was unmoved. I was ready for a fight. I liked the pose, for one thing. I was a tough guy, see? No one gets me to cop a plea. I'm tougher than those creeps. Go ahead, give me your best shot. I'll beat you and your whole team, Walsh. In addition, the fight would be fascinating, and it would be all-consuming. I wasn't doing anything all that fascinating right then: my book on U.S. foreign policy was written, and the combination of writing, thinking, and consulting I was then undertaking did not thrill me. A trial would be terrifically interesting.

And then there was the Fiers problem with a plea. Fiers had apparently incriminated his former superior, Clair George. Everyone would assume I had also incriminated someone in any plea I made, would assume I was an informant, a stoolie. "Cooperating with the investigation." "Turned state's evidence." Disgusting.

And Rachel wanted to fight. Her hatred of these prosecutors was pure, white-hot. She wanted to strike back against them, and against the entire corrupt system they represented: of congressmen who had conspired with the Sandinistas. Of staff people who had leaked secret documents to reporters. Of reporters who had written vicious, biased stories about me. Of Reagan Administration officials who had gone on to their glory and had left me and a few others out there on the beach to take the incoming fire.

She had no way to fight them, except this: we would tell them go fuck yourselves, no plea, go ahead and indict, and we will kick your faces in court. Your worst defeat won't be the North case. It will be the Abrams case.

TUESDAY, OCTOBER 1

Point Man or Front Man?

I began the day meeting with a client, and I deserved an Oscar for my performance: calm and collected, apparently devoting all my mental attention to the client's interests. And I was, in a way, for it provided a wonderful form of escape.

Life was now virtually suspended. I made no commitments: no lunch appointments, no dinners, no speeches, no nothing. I ducked phone calls. I had a folder on my desk marked "AFTER," and I threw into it every letter that concerned any future event. The "future" consisted of the next three or four days. The end of history was October 10, when the statute of limitations ran out.

What do you tell friends? You quickly make a mental cut: those you tell, those you don't. And what do you tell the ones you tell? Mostly, that Walsh is after you and you don't know how it will turn out. For a few, more truth: it looks bad, they seem intent on indicting. You say it calmly, because you've said it before, you are bathing in it. People are shocked, and you realize how shocking it is. It *is* shocking. It's also very interesting, so people want to talk about it. They are amazed at your calm. What can we do to help? they ask. There is nothing.

President Bush and President Reagan are not among my personal friends, so they do not call, they do not say, "What can I do? Anything I can do to help?" I do not have the chance to say, Oh, yes. Fire Walsh. Pardon everyone. Stop calculating the political effect, start worrying about people's lives.

Why did Reagan do this? Go back to 1986. North and Poindexter had been fired. Congress had announced a huge, giant, juicy investigation into Iran/Contra, and the Administration had announced the Tower Commission. Hadn't that been enough? Couldn't they have held off on a Special Prosecutor until those investigations were over, until the political firestorm had begun to burn out? No, it was all politics. Make the President seem alarmed, wanting the whole truth out, wanting to do all he can, no stone unturned. Had there been no one, not one single person, to tell him "Don't do it?" No one to say, it will turn on a machine that will never turn itself off, a scandal machine, a machine controlled by your political enemies, a machine that will justify itself by the number of victims it creates, a machine that wants revenge, not justice? No one?

And then, no Christmas pardons in 1988, when Reagan was beyond revenge and Bush already elected? And then, nothing from the new President, who could have said "enough is enough"?

Stop moping, I told myself. If you can't stand the heat, you shouldn't have jumped into the kitchen. But I withstood the heat of the kitchen, I told myself. Only they never said they would incinerate the kitchen, they never said the kitchen would become ground zero for a nuclear blast, they never said everyone who had been near the kitchen would become radioactive.

I spent hours that day reading a new book, just out, about the Contras' human rights abuses and U.S. efforts to stop them. The book said the problem of human rights abuses in the Contra camps in Honduras had been serious; the State Department had tried hard to stop the abuses and have the abusers punished; the CIA had deceived the State Department, blunted its efforts, protected its "assets."

I was disgusted. The book appeared to be accurate, so far as I could judge, and its accounts of things I remembered were right. I was disgusted that my "colleagues" at CIA had apparently undercut us right and left. We would argue endlessly in and out of the RIG, would finally reach agreement, a decent compromise on how to proceed, and then they wouldn't proceed. Or worse yet, they would tell me they had, when they hadn't. Also, the abuses seemed worse than I had known. Much worse.

The book might be useful, it showed a pattern of CIA deception of me which should remind Walsh and Gillen that I was a victim, not a perpetrator. What North knew, what Fiers knew, should not be attributed to me. They kept secrets from me. I sent copies of the book to my lawyers with little notes, with key pages marked. Can this help? Will Walsh understand the point?

The book gave State a lot of credit, some for ending human rights abuses and lots for trying. But who was State? The book mentioned many of my subordinates, acting under my instructions on these issues I had cared so much about. I had gone to the Latin America job from the Human Rights bureau, from being Assistant Secretary of State for Human Rights and Humanitarian Affairs. Yet, predictably, I got no credit. It was asking too much from the author, a *Miami Herald* journalist, to say something nice about Elliott Abrams. The Left wouldn't like that. I was not furious, because this was not new. I had spent three and a half years at the Human Rights Bureau, and there were people out there in Haiti or El Salvador or Chile who knew the true story. But no journalist would ever write it. I had been the point man on Central America, the key guy behind the Contras, and that was that. No one would ever say to this author, hey, your book is ridiculous, don't you know that Abrams was behind all the stuff you are so very keen on? The press had the view of history that had survived so long in Moscow: if you didn't like it, it had never happened. So why report it?

On the other hand, what the book did say made me sick. I had been misled, fooled, bamboozled, tricked, and deceived by my colleagues, my handlers, at CIA. Walsh could say whatever he wanted about my relations with North and Fiers, but he would never even see the issue that meant the most to me. I understood politics and ideology better than Fiers or North, I was higher-ranking, and I had Shultz behind me when I needed him. *So how had all this happened?* Why had I not pressed Fiers to the wall when I needed to?

Why had I not insisted on knowing *everything* the Agency was up to? Why was I learning now, in 1991, about things I should have known about in 1985 or 1986?

That, to me, was my failing. I was supposed to be the point man, not the front man. I was supposed to be leading the NSC and CIA efforts, not providing cover for them.

There was one explanation: I had been new. I had not been a career operative, a career diplomat, a career soldier, and I had had to learn the hard way. And some things I had never learned, like taking the "information" colleagues gave me with a large grain of salt, like assuming I was being misled half the time.

If I had it to do over again, I would be as tough with the CIA and NSC as I had been with the congressmen. I would use the National Security Agency, the Defense Intelligence Agency, the Intelligence Committees, and moles of my own wherever I could find a friend, to find out what was really going on, who was behind what, who was withholding what from me, and why.

Except, who wanted a next time? The more I learned, the more disgusted I was.

My father-in-law has a wonderful saying: "No good deed goes unpunished." This was my experience.

For me there was no credit for the human rights campaigns, but plenty of vicious personal attacks for having tried to stop Communism in Nicaragua. And now it seemed there had been more corruption and violence within the Contra leadership—not the troops, who were peasants and farmers fighting to win back their country, but the leaders with whom the United States had worked—than I had known. And here was a new book about the pattern of deception of State by CIA.

On and on it went, and I thought, what "next time"? Who would volunteer for more of this? I was following the Gates hearings and the Clarence Thomas hearings closely, and my disgust deepened. Who were these pious clowns beating Gates up every day on TV? Most of them had been on the Senate Intelligence Committee when I was testifying there about Central America, and I remembered them well. The ones who had never cared enough to show up, not until the cameras were there. The ones whose questions, in closed session, had been so abysmally stupid, I would save them up each time for my wife, to give her a good laugh.

Metzenbaum, the multimillionaire involved in one squalid commercial dispute after another, thinking nothing of lecturing Gates, as he had lectured me, on morality!

And Ted Kennedy, and Joe Biden, and Metzenbaum again, sitting in judgment upon Clarence Thomas, a man accused and abused without a semblance of fair procedure. Wow, I thought, what country is this?

And I answered, it is Washington. In America, it may be that these things still do not happen. I had, after leaving the government in January 1989, wanted to get back into it. I had wondered if, after the statute of limitations had run, I might try, at least with some National Commission, some part-time, honorary thing. I had known it would be a while before I could be confirmed for anything by the Senate, maybe five or ten more years; and maybe never. And that had hurt. But now, now it no longer hurt. I was revolted by the idea. For the first time, I realized I would really, seriously tell a young man or woman interested in politics to stay home, to tend their own gardens. At worst, if they couldn't shake the urge, run for Governor. Stay out of Washington.

Meanwhile, the Elliott Abrams Diet was a continuing success. Every day my pants were bigger, my belts were longer.

THURSDAY, OCTOBER 3

"I Am Not Going to Plead"

The day got off to a bright start: a friend from the White House staff called to say there was a rumor circulating. Boyden Gray, the White House Counsel, had apparently heard that I was going to be indicted the following day. Good news travels fast, I thought, but I told my friend there was nothing I could say.

Pierson returned to Washington, met with Walsh and Gillen, and then reported to me and to the rest of the crew. Walsh would still not meet with Levine and Morgan, and in addition Gillen had had the nerve to complain to Pierson about a press story referring to Barry Levine as my lawyer. It wasn't enough that they were prohibiting me from having Levine attend meetings, by Gillen's lights. I couldn't even see him, or speak to him. What was the Sixth Amendment to a Special Prosecutor, after all? Gillen was "testy," Pierson reported. I was infuriated.

And it was costing me money. Everything had to be prepared for at greater length than usual, and then reported back in detail to everyone. Moreover, I was gravely disadvantaged by the absence of my criminal lawyers, with all their experience, from those meetings with Walsh.

Walsh had told Pierson the grand jury was meeting the next day, Friday, but he would be willing to postpone it until Monday if we wanted more time to think. He had not said, "We will indict Mr. Abrams tomorrow," but that was implicit. Pierson had not asked for a postponement but had made the case, yet again, for our side. He had taken his time, covered all the bases, and covered them carefully. We had discussed it in advance, we had marshaled the arguments again during long talks among all of us, taxi meter running at full speed, and now he had turned the full force of our logic, the facts, and his own personality and experience on them.

Walsh's response was bizarre. There are some things I'd like to know, he had said. How did Elliott get this job, to begin with? Why, Shultz asked him to take it, Pierson had replied. Elliott had asked for the top AID job, but it wasn't available, and Shultz asked him to take this one. Walsh wondered if it were not extraordinary to give someone with my background this job, to ask someone without diplomatic experience to oversee all those embassies at such a hot time. Oh yes, Pierson had said, thinking there might be an opportunity here. Elliott had had no experience dealing with the CIA, with covert operations in the field. Well, who was his sponsor, Walsh had asked, back in 1981? How did he get into the Administration? Pierson had not known.

This was curious. Did they think maybe William J. Casey had gotten me the initial job in 1981, and were they looking for such a link?

Walsh had then asked Pierson how the reporting relationships had gone in my bureau. Had every ambassador reported to and through me? Had anyone had a separate, private pipeline to the Seventh Floor, where Shultz sat? No. That was specifically forbidden, and all ambassadors were told to report to and through the Assistant Secretary. Well, Walsh had asked, how did Elliott deal with the career ambassadors? How did he know how to deal with them? He got advice, Pierson had replied, from his deputies, most of whom were career foreign service officers. Was Elliott cut out? Walsh had wanted to know. Was there a pipeline around him? To Shultz? Pierson had not thought so.

To us Pierson said, boy, they sure would like to get Shultz.

It was not clear to me what this was all about. Did they think my own guys had misled or misinformed me? Did they think I had been

kept out of things by people who were, at least on paper, my subordinates? Did they think Shultz had done something wrong? This was
all, in a despicable way, mildly encouraging, for if they thought all
this, maybe they thought I wasn't guilty. Or maybe they were just
trying to give me hints about what might be a good proffer.

I do believe Elliott was hung out to dry in many ways, Walsh had
continued. Yes, Pierson had replied, both from above and from below.
His greatest loyalty was to George Shultz, but Shultz never told him
about the Saudi money, and a lot of the testimony you dislike most
would have been avoided if he had known about that. And maybe
others did not tell him the whole story either; you have plenty of
memos showing meetings he never attended.

Well, Walsh had said, I have spent a lot of time thinking about an
alternative disposition. I talked to Abe Sofaer, and he raised it with
me. But I think it would appear so contrived. And some possible
results would actually be more onerous than those likely to follow
pleading to a misdemeanor charge.

We had in fact spent lots of time trying to think up noncriminal
alternatives, and there weren't too many. Some statutes provide for
civil penalties, fines, or injunctions; the ones we were dealing with
here did not. Still, the answer rankled. It would appear "contrived"?
The use of 1001—the false testimony statute—in policy disputes for
the first time in two hundred years of American history, that was not
"contrived"? The use of 2 USC 192—the contempt of Congress statute—in the Fiers case, without a contempt citation by Congress, having Fiers waive the citation—that was not "contrived"?

Well, Pierson had proposed, how about a joint statement? We had
thought up this idea before the meeting with Walsh. If you indict
Elliott, the argument went, he will attack you and this office, and so
will a lot of other people. It will be considered so highly political. It's
just days before the statute of limitations runs. It's just days after you
lost the North case. And he was not in any way involved in the Iran
side of things, and would be the first defendant who was not. And you
know, you can lose this case, and with that loss destroy much of what
you are trying to build here. Isn't this office better off avoiding that,
and instead getting a statement from Elliott saying, thank you for not

prosecuting me, you are a fine and generous bunch of people, I made some terrible mistakes, I am so sorry about them?

Walsh had seemed to waver. He was unsure. He had asked for a delay, a chance to caucus with Craig Gillen. Meanwhile, he had said to Pierson, you think about everything you said to me this morning, and think about my responsibilities as well, and be prepared to tell me what you would do if you were in my shoes.

Walsh and Gillen had left the room for twenty minutes. I don't know what happened, and Pierson doesn't know, and we'll both never know. But I know what I think: I think Walsh had been about to give it up, and Gillen had pushed him back. Maybe that's all wrong, maybe Walsh's "I am a humanitarian" bit, his indecision, his effort to understand my arguments, had all been an act. Perhaps he had wished to *appear* fair, without meaning actually to *be* fair. But I don't think so; I think that at that moment he would have said yes, and Gillen turned him around.

They had returned to the conference room, and Walsh had asked Pierson to say his piece. If I were Independent Counsel, Pierson had said, I would want to be careful never to bring charges unless conviction were *likely*. You can lose a case like this, and that loss would be devastating to this office. I would insist on specific evidence of criminal intent, or I would not proceed. You have a CIPA problem here, too. Quite right: the Classified Information Procedures Act had gotten Joe Fernandez, the CIA man in Costa Rica, off the hook, because his defense had required lots of classified documents the government had been unwilling to give him. Well, Walsh had said, I understand that problem, and I have never shrunk from it before.

I would look very hard, Pierson had continued, at the issue of proportionality of conduct, and comparative culpability, among people like Poindexter, North, Fiers, George, McFarlane, and Abrams. If Fiers, who knew about the Iran diversion and was much deeper into this than Elliott, deserves a misdemeanor count, Elliott deserves less. Oh, well, Walsh had interjected, Fiers earned his misdemeanor count; he made a spectacular proffer. (Yeah, I thought, when Pierson recounted this: Clair George's future.) It is critical, Pierson had gone on, for the survival and integrity of the Independent Counsel process that this office be able to show restraint, that you be able to refute the powerful criticism today that you get so wrapped up in one matter you never decline prosecution, even where a normal U.S. Attorney would. And, if I were Independent Counsel I would want to give very serious consideration to a disposition involving a public statement by Elliott, *now,* that would indicate you had played fair with him, that the normal procedures of our government had been prostituted and were now being set right. That would be a very powerful statement to this office, and it would be unavailable in a criminal context.

And then, Pierson had concluded, there is the human side. You know what this branding means to someone. You know how it will affect his life. You should not do it. I would not do it; I would not prosecute.

Powerful stuff, I thought, and powerfully presented. If Walsh were not the village idiot, why would he not say yes? I knew why, of course: he needed scalps. Not statements, not justice, scalps. Still, there was a real chance here. This was so right, so fair; maybe Pierson could prevail.

Nope.

Walsh had replied, I want to say to you that the difference we have between us is that we think the case we would bring is a lot narrower and a lot simpler than you do, judging by all the matters we discussed this morning. I do believe Elliott was caught in the middle. But in the course of that, he made false statements that he knew were false. I believe Craig will be able to prove that to the jury—and because I believe that, I cannot accept your conclusion.

And look, he had continued, a misdemeanor count isn't so onerous, so terrible a burden. Now is the perfect time to get rid of this; why, with all that Clarence Thomas stuff on TV, all that Gates stuff, this will hardly make a ripple. Oh, Judge, Pierson had replied, the papers will find room for this item. They'll find some room. But now is the time to ring down the curtain, Walsh had said—now. If you would like additional time, we can delay the grand jury from tomorrow until Monday. Talk to Elliott. Call us back. Should we delay the grand jury?

Thus Pierson reported to us, and "us" was now a wider group: it included Rachel. She had realized we were getting down to the final decision now, and she ought to be there. Of course, the final decision had already been made, at least in theory. I was going to fight. No pleas. My mother had come around, too; she could tell from my voice what I wanted to do and how I felt, and if I thought that was the right route, she was for it.

We met in one of the Dickstein, Shapiro conference rooms, a small one, crowded with the six of us: Rachel and me, Garment, Levine, Morgan, Pierson.

All right. They will probably indict; it looks as if they will indict tomorrow, we all agreed. They will not buy a noncriminal disposition.

So the choices are, plead or fight. Fight means a year, two if you need an appeal, and the legal fee will be over a million dollars. If you lose, you go to jail. Pleading means pleading to one misdemeanor count, perhaps dealing with Brunei, which is the testimony where you've already admitted withholding information, and that means you won't be disbarred, probably would get what McFarlane got. Maybe less. He got a $25,000 fine and two hundred hours of community service. Which he didn't hate: he worked with disabled Vietnam vets and found the work very fulfilling. Want to talk to him? Or to Richard Helms?

No. I just wanted to talk to Rachel. And she was getting tired of this roomful of lawyers. Taken one by one, she liked each of them very much. She was very grateful to them for all they were doing for me. Taken together, they were a bad influence, she felt. If that taxi meter I kept imagining were on a stand, like a bubblegum machine, she would have picked it up and thrown it at them. All this legal mumbo-jumbo, when the issues were much clearer, much more profound. It wasn't a matter of Section 1001 and 2 USC 192 and CIPA and non-criminal dispositions. It was a matter of justice, of fairness. It was a matter of her husband, the father of her children, and what those filthy, rotten animals were doing to us. She bridled when anyone suggested, even implied, even hinted, that Walsh had been reasonable about something. When pleas were mentioned, she rebelled: why are we talking about pleas again? I thought we had decided that, she would say. She did not want reasonable talk about all the options, not just

UNDUE PROCESS

then, no lawyer talk. This was about far more primal matters than lawyers knew how to deal with; it was about people trying to crush her husband, annihiliate him, smash him, and for the very worst reasons. Political reasons, because I had championed a policy the Establishment had decided to abandon, and personal reasons, because the prosecutors needed a scalp. Welcome to Washington, Your Nation's Capital.

We asked the lawyers to give us some time together, and we sat alone in the conference room and talked. Well, this is it. Time for the decision. Rachel had a clear view. Those people are your enemies, and you should not capitulate to them. You should not surrender. And pleading guilty means capitulating. You just can't.

I agreed. Then we talked about money, and how things would be hard. Maybe we could raise a million dollars through direct mail, as North had done. Maybe we could raise half of it. Barry Levine would see us through, he wouldn't abandon us. The larger problem is, what do we live on?

And what about the kids? Oh, I said, it will be a hell of a lot easier to explain this, fighting, than it would ever be to explain pleading. This way, I'll say to them, people are accusing me of something. Of lying. And I did not. So I am saying, No I didn't, and now we will have a big court case. They understand that in a minute: when you are unjustly accused, you defend yourself.

What if I go to jail? Peter says that if I lose, I go to jail. We won't lose, Rachel said. Well, I agree, I said, but we might. Look, she said, nothing that can happen here will destroy our family or our marriage. Nothing. This is not death, this is not disease, we will get through it. Any of it. All of it.

It took only twenty minutes, twenty minutes of splendid quiet, of splendid isolation. Rachel sat in my lap and we hugged and kissed like teenagers on a date, and wondered what would happen if one of our lawyers barged in. Then we called them back, and I said, Well, I am scared to death of going to jail, but we are going to fight. I am not going to plead.

Okay.

With the decision made, Rachel said she would leave, for she had to pick up the kids.

Wait: Peter Morgan had an idea. A great idea. A brilliant idea. A perfect idea.

Look, he said, they want a criminal disposition. And you don't want a criminal conviction. *There is a middle road here,* there is a compromise. Under the federal criminal procedures, there is what is known as "pretrial diversion." A typical case involves a first-time drug offender. The guy goes into court, and either a criminal charge is filed, and the judge then suspends entering a plea and a conviction pending the pretrial proceedings, or no charge is actually even filed. So you do not have a criminal record. You have no conviction. Instead, you are hooked up with the U.S. Probation Service, and you do some kind of community service under their auspices.

It was perfect. Walsh wanted me in the criminal justice system; I would enter the criminal justice system. If need be, if he absolutely insisted, he could even formally charge me. I would make a nice statement saying how sorry I was about everything, and how fairly the Independent Control had treated me, and I would do the community service. It's supposed to be something suited to your training and background, so I proposed working for the Legal Aid Society. I was enthusiastic about it, because I could actually learn something of trial practice, at long last, after fifteen years away from the small bit of litigation I had done on Wall Street after law school.

How much community service? Look, Peter said, this is the inducement for Walsh, it's got to be heavy. It's got to be something he can sink his teeth into. A thousand hours. Whew; that is six months, I thought, and if you do it part-time it could take a couple of years. Okay. A thousand hours. Has a catchy sound.

And I wanted to learn to be a lawyer again. Not the bad kind of lawyer, not the Lawrence-Walsh-Wall-Street-Neutron-Bomb type, but the kind that deals with people in trouble. Criminal defendants. In law school everyone who does this kind of community service ends up disillusioned and tells his roommate late at night, "I didn't think they'd all be guilty." That was okay with me. Just learning it would be fascinating, I was sure I'd be good at it, and anyway, who is the enemy when you do criminal defense? Prosecutors! Right. Think of it, fighting and beating prosecutors! I couldn't wait. Okay, a thousand hours.

UNDUE PROCESS

Rachel left. Peter went off to draw up the papers on pretrial diversion that Pierson would present to Walsh. Pierson called Walsh and said, put the grand jury over until Monday; there is something worth talking about. I sat down and drafted the statement I would make when I entered the pretrial diversion program.

I was happy. I was always happy when I had made a decision; the only thing that depressed me and made me nervous was indecision. Now, Rachel would have put it differently: when I was with the family I was happy, but the goddamn lawyers were always raising "issues," reopening decisions, creating problems. No decision was ever a decision, there was always something more, something else, something new. It was never, fight your enemies. It was never, this is good and that is evil. Those words were not part of the lawyer's lexicon, whereas good and evil were the key concepts in Rachel's moral universe.

So whenever I came out of a meeting with the lawyers I was confused, intellectually and maybe even morally. But now Rachel and I were of one mind, and we could deal with the indictment. And Peter had come up with a fabulous idea, so the escape hatch was open.

I sat and read through the federal sentencing guidelines, page after page after page, trying to figure out what my sentence would be if convicted of perjury, false testimony, or obstruction of justice. It's a complicated point system: points for your crime, more points for hurting victims, points off for confessing or having a lesser role in the crime, or having no criminal record. I sat there wondering if the point system would say, three points off because you never treated your President as a dunce, never saw it as your job to compromise or desert or undercut his policies, never tried to show the Democrats you thought this Reaganism–Conservatism stuff was nonsense and we were all in it for power and publicity and we could work it all out, all us pals playing the Washington game. Did you get two points off if you didn't use your job to set up some lucrative consulting contracts, didn't crawl around from bank to bank, oil company to oil company greasing your future bankrollers? Or did they add five points for stupidity, my kind of stupidity, the stupidity of someone who poured his whole career into Nicaragua—Nicaragua! and was now sitting in a lawyer's office reading the federal sentencing guidelines?

UNDUE PROCESS

Then I thought, sitting alone in the conference room, I have figured out a better sentence. How about *banishment*! Lots of precedent for that one, going back to the Bible and right through to the New England colonies. That's it: Walsh should banish me. In the Human Rights Bureau we had dealt with some cases of it in Zaïre, where they called it rustication. You had to leave Kinshasa and go back to some village without electricity or running water or croissants.

They could banish me from Washington, to . . . to . . . where? Omaha? Tulsa? Buffalo? This was it, the perfect sentence. Now this would be justice, this would be the way for Washington to punish those who had broken its elaborate code of behavior. Where greasing your bank account was okay, betraying your President was okay, leaking classified documents was okay, almost anything was okay, except defying the Democrats on the Hill and insisting on pushing and pushing and pushing for the Contras. That was not okay, and now you had to pay the penalty: you could not go to Kay Graham's house for dinner any more, you could not lunch at the Palm, you would not be quoted in the *Post*. Bob Strauss would not shake your hand on K Street. Some men would die first. I thought I would survive.

I had been amazed at the virulence of the opposition my behavior aroused, but when I reread all my testimony I was less surprised. Talk about *lese majesté*! I used to joke with friends: they have accused me of a hundred crimes I did not commit; the only crime I probably committed was contempt of Congress. Ha ha, great line. Many chuckles. But it was there in the transcripts: they had played hardball and I had played it too. Sometimes the hearings had been models of good questioning, good dialogue, but sometimes they had been open warfare. And I had given as good as I got. And they had hated it. They had hated it when I said to Foreign Relations Committee members who asked about intelligence matters, ''Congressman, you're on the wrong committee, you ought to get yourself on the Intelligence Committee.'' When I said to John Kerry, ''Listen to me, Senator; you're not listening.'' You weren't supposed to talk like that to the Congress of the United States, no matter how much check-kiting or colluding with a Communist embassy they were doing, no matter *what* they were doing. Even if Jim Wright had been off signing book contracts, even if staff

UNDUE PROCESS

guys had been working with the Sandinistas against the Administration, even if Congressmen had virtually accused you of being in league with drug traffickers and arms traffickers and murderers and torturers. No matter what *they* said, you were not to reply in kind. That was not done. There was a price to pay. And it was not going to be banishment.

I saw that, under the point system, I would go to jail if I were convicted, but Peter's plan was too good. How could they reject it? They'd have gotten me into the criminal justice system, and with a thousand-hour penalty. Versus Bud McFarlane's two hundred, after pleading guilty. They'd be nuts to reject it.

My lawyers heard my conclusion and told me to watch it: Walsh would not buy this, most likely. It wasn't used for these cases, and some of the criteria didn't exactly fit. Don't start getting optimistic, the lawyers said. Okay, okay, I nodded. But the guidelines fitted if you wanted them to fit. That, we all agreed on; it wasn't too much of a stretch. The pretrial diversion procedures didn't apply to "violations of the public trust" by officials or to "foreign policy and national security" cases. I had read that language too, but this was not "violation of the public trust," a phrase used to describe fraud and other financial crimes where an official uses his job to put money in his pocket; neither was it a "foreign policy" matter like treason, for it involved the most domestic crime conceivable, a contempt of Congress case, or a 1001 case. Anyway, where there's a will, there's a way. And Jesus Christ, Walsh had broken every rule in the book, had spit on precedents, had invented crimes that would have put Franklin Roosevelt in Alcatraz. So if he wanted to do this, he could. Who could stop him?

Meanwhile, I added and subtracted points. And I wondered where they'd send me if I went to prison. Would I meet Michael Milken and Ivan Boesky? Maybe they'd like me and offer to pay my legal fees. Or give me stock tips. Maybe I'd get my own cell, and if they let me have a computer I could write a book. During that idyllic California July, driving from San Francisco to Los Angeles, Rachel and I had driven right by Lompoc, the federal prison farm, and had joked about my coming to stay there. Wasn't there one in Florida, too, where white-collar criminals went? Maybe I could be a jailhouse lawyer, and all the Mafiosi would ask my advice and send Rachel theater tickets, two on the aisle, first row, the way Frank Costello had once done for Edward Bennett Williams. But this was all idle thinking, because Peter's idea was *so* good, so terrific, they just had to buy it. So there would be no indictment, maybe; maybe there would be no two-year fight, no million-dollar fees, no risk of jail. Maybe. It was a chance, a relief, an escape, and mentally and emotionally, I jumped at it.

FRIDAY, OCTOBER 4

Time to End It

P ierson went off to his appointment with Walsh and Gillen, armed with the papers we had prepared. We had followed the Federal Rules of Criminal Procedure religiously, everything was ready, and I had even prepared the statement I would make. A terrific statement, one that I could honestly subscribe to and that would be of enormous use to Walsh. In it, I said this was no way to conduct a foreign policy. Stealth leads to more stealth, deception to more deception—and to working with people who have lived their lives in the shadows. The Independent Counsel's investigation had shown just how much had gone wrong, how much the normal processes of government had been abused. This was all true, and I could say it. And I went on and apologized for withholding information, for testimony that did not give Congress all the information it needed to fulfill its constitutional role. I could say this, too, although not without a bitter aftertaste. But I could say it.

Pierson presented it all, including the statement, and he started by saying, Elliott is prepared to enter the criminal justice system, but in a way that we think is fairer to him. When the meeting was over, hours

119

and hours later, he returned and we all met at Garment's office again, in the same small conference room, only this time without Rachel.

Walsh, Pierson reported, had gone through all the papers. Then he had said, "It looks like we're getting close." I knew it! They couldn't say no. But wait: Walsh and Gillen had once again gone off, and had left Pierson sitting there, this time for a whole hour. Then they had returned, and Walsh had said, we're so taken with the effort you're making, I've talked to the Justice Department and other offices about it all. But we just can't take this kind of case to pretrial diversion. We did not dismiss it out of hand, but we just can't square this with the eligibility criteria. We would be criticized if we tried to do this, and anyway we ourselves don't think it fits.

Well, Pierson had said—one last college try—let's do it outside the formal pretrial diversion process. We can just do it. Same statement by Elliott, same commitment to a thousand hours, same restraint by you on prosecuting him; the only difference is, he doesn't have a probation officer.

Oh no, we couldn't do that, Walsh had answered. That would be too hokey. I looked it up later: "hokey" means "sickly or affectedly sentimental; obviously contrived."

Well, sure, I could understand that, I could sympathize. I wouldn't want Judge Walsh to be criticized. I wouldn't want him to have to reach, to stretch, just to avoid wrenching my life out of shape. The man who is praised and denounced in newspapers every day, why, he couldn't be expected to court the mortal peril of being fair to Elliott Abrams. The man who invented new crimes, who used 1001 for the *first time in American history* in a policy dispute, he couldn't be expected to do that. The man who fought the Justice Department on issue after issue, whose independence from the rest of the government was an obvious point of pride to him, why, he couldn't be expected to make his own decision on a central matter of national destiny like whether the pretrial diversion guidelines could be stretched to fit me.

Walsh was not a Calvinist, I concluded, devoted to doing what he thought right regardless of the criticism it might elicit; instead, he was a man whose sense of justice depended on the approval of the *New York Times,* a man whose staff pushed him around. And for them, this was politics, this was ambition: Craig Gillen's chance to fill the scrapbook, to start building the career that would lead to the stars. Game over.

Now it hit me. For the first time. Again. These things come in waves: you believe they'll indict you, then you don't believe it. You realize what is going to happen, then you believe in an escape. Each time is the first time. But this wave was a bigger wave, and I was being dragged under now, for real. Tut-tutting about their fairness and about The Law, and saying this way out was not fitting and that way out was hokey, they were holding my head under. And all the while, with their pained smiles that said, Oh this hurts us, you know, we get no pleasure from his, Oh it is so unfortunate. Judge Walsh is eighty, you know, and his wife is back in Oklahoma City and is not well, and he goes back there every weekend, but he couldn't go this weekend, he's staying here to work on this matter personally. Just as he did last weekend. Two in a row, because of this matter. Well I am really touched, I thought, I am really moved. The sacrifices he is making just to make sure Elliott Abrams doesn't escape his net. What a great American!

We think we have a strong case, Walsh had told Pierson. Now, we really liked Elliott very much; he dispelled lots of impressions that had been formed about him. But we don't view a misdemeanor as a harsh result, given our evidence. We are convinced we have a sound felony case.

Walsh had, that morning, asked about cooperation, and Pierson in response had asked what Walsh meant by cooperation. We mean, is he bound by past testimony? Walsh had answered. In future talks with us, would he be governed by what is true, or by his past testimony? They didn't believe I was telling the truth, and whatever it meant to say that "we really like Elliott very much," it did not mean that they thought I wasn't a liar. What was I, then? A nice liar? A liar they liked? So they thought I was not telling the truth, but about what? That was not clear.

I reject this "weight of the evidence" charge, this kind of non-specific allegation, Pierson had replied. You should not base a felony charge on that kind of evidence. Oh, we're not, Walsh had said, we have evidence; we have a strong case. I was mystified. How in hell did they think they could ever prove I had known of any illegal activity, had ever thought Oliver North actually ran, directed, and managed the private network? They had absolutely no evidence of that. Would North say it? I didn't believe he would, and if he did, that meant their key witness was someone who hated Walsh bitterly, whom Walsh had labeled a liar. Would Fiers say it? This was equally improbable to me, but Fiers was now awaiting sentencing. Would their only witness be someone who had never said these things before and was only saying them now while the government was trying to decide what sentence to give him? That was their "strong case" of perjury, obstruction of justice, 1001 violations?

Then Gillen had spoken. I have listened to you and to Mr. Abrams, he had said, and I have to tell you that in my view you are defending the wrong bright line regarding his testimony defining North's operational role. Gillen's term "bright line" was a lawyer's term, an expression I had learned in law school, and it meant a sharp, clear, important distinction. We don't have to show that he understood North's operational role, Gillen had continued. We think we can, but we don't need to. We will be able to show the jury his October 10, 1986, testimony, and we will be able to show them inconsistent testimony regarding the extent of Mr. Abrams's knowledge.

You should look at his October 10 testimony, Gillen had gone on, in the context of his other statements; look at page eleven, for example. Abrams admits enough about North, enough knowledge about North: not that he knew North had an operational role, not that he knew North was doing anything unlawful—okay?—but the Congress was asking about the extent of government involvement, not whether it was lawful or not, and they were entitled to know the extent of government involvement, even if it was lawful involvement. Mr. Abrams knew there was *some* kind of government involvement, and he said there wasn't any. We think we have a good false statement and obstruction case.

Pierson finished telling the story to all of us in the conference room, and stopped. There was a pause in the room, and it felt to me like a tremendous blast of cold air had rushed in.

Gillen had not even mentioned perjury. He had not said they were sure they could prove I knew North ran the private network, or knew

North had ever done anything illegal. I thought he was saying, if you worked it all the way through, Look, we'll throw all these false statement charges at the jury, all these obstruction charges, all these felony counts, and we'll show that you denied *everything*. You denied any connection to the private network, any U.S. Government tie at all. And maybe we'll convince all the jurors you were lying, and maybe we'll only convince one or two or three, and maybe it will confuse all of them. But we'll put on witness after witness suggesting you had to know *something,* it was in the air, everyone knew something was up, and even if all our evidence is circumstantial, all of it, and no document or witness ties you to any particular knowledge, it will be enough. The jury, or some of the jurors, will think you must have known something about ties to the U.S. Government. So they compromise. We have ten or fifteen counts, they settle on just one or two.

And then, I said to myself, I go to jail.

A very fine theory Mr. Gillen had come up with. He was smart. A good prosecutor. We can't prove what we think, but we'll throw enough at the jury to get them to do something. That was how I read his strategy.

First question: what had I actually said? What was this page eleven?

On October 10, 1986, I had testified to the Senate Foreign Relations Committee. I had been asked about a *Los Angeles Times* article that had appeared that morning. The article reported an elaborate system of private support for the Contras and alleged that U.S. officials had run it. I was asked to comment on the article and the charge, and here is what I said:

> In the last two years, since Congress cut off support to the Resistance, this supply system has kept them alive. It is not our supply system. It is one that grew up after we were forbidden from supplying the Resistance, and we have been kind of careful not to get closely involved with it and to stay away from it. . . .
>
> I think that people who are supplying the Contras believe that we generally approve of what they are doing—and they are right. We do generally approve of what they are doing, because they are keeping

the Contras alive while Congress makes its decision, which each House has separately, though obviously final legislation is not yet ready.

So, the notion that we are generally in favor of people helping the Contras is correct.

We do not encourage people to do this. We don't round up people, we don't write letters, we don't have conversations, we don't tell them to do this, we don't ask them to do it. But I think it is quite clear, from the attitude of the Administration, the attitude of the Administration is that these people are doing a very good thing, and if they think they are doing something that we like, then, in a general sense, they are right. But that is without any encouragement and coordination from us, other than a public speech by the President, that kind of thing, on the public record.

On October 14, I had been asked in a hearing of the House Intelligence Committee on the Hasenfus flight, "Can anybody assure us that the United States Government was not involved, directly or indirectly, in any way in the supply of the Contras?" And I had said, "I believe we have already done that, that is, I think, the President has done it, the Secretary has done it." "So the answer is the United States Government was not involved in any way," the Chairman had asked, and I had replied, "The answer to your question is yes."

On October 15, I had been asked about the U.S. Government role in the Hasenfus flight by the House Foreign Affairs Committee, and I had replied, "There is a great deal of information which I cannot reveal at an open hearing. . . . It doesn't relate to any of this which I have flatly denied and which is false—these charges of U.S. Government involvement."

So the denial was pretty flat. What had I said to contradict the denial? I had told the Tower Board in January 1987: "We knew that there were outside benefactors. . . . I think it is fair to say that everybody involved in the RIG knew that Ollie was somehow connected with this but did not know how." I had told them "Ollie . . . had the most information about this private network." I had repeated all that in the Iran/Contra hearings in June 1987. I had said I thought North had the best ties to the private network, and I had said that he received information from them. I had testified that, after the Hasenfus plane was shot down, North had told me Hasenfus's employers, the people who operated the flight, had called him. I had testified that he knew who some of the contributors to the private network were, and knew how to reach them. I had once asked him about reaching out to them to get some money to pay for bringing home to the United States the bodies of the two Americans who had died on the Hasenfus flight.

Well, then, Gillen was saying, you knew there were conversations. You knew there was some kind of interaction, interchange, connection, relationship, involvement, *something*.

This was ridiculous, I told the lawyers: Everyone knew *that,* that's not what I was really being asked. I knew what the congressmen meant. They obviously meant, was there any *illegal* activity? Was there any *operational* role? All their questions were within the context of the Boland Amendment and charges that we were violating it. And it was the same on fundraising. I knew what they had meant. They were asking if the Contras were being funded then, or had ever been funded, by a foreign government, and I answered "No" because that was what I believed, and the Brunei pledge had not yet resulted in one cent in cash. Not yet.

Peter Morgan spoke. This was a problem. They had garbage evidence when it came to convincing a jury that I knew or thought anyone was breaking the law, that anyone was violating Boland, that North was running this operation. But this was different. My words were pretty clear, they had a plain meaning. I had said, no connections, no conversations. But there had been conversations between North and the private network, and I had known it. Maybe everyone had known it, but that wasn't going to help me.

North had had this problem in his trial, too. Some of the things he had said were hard to swallow, and he had admitted it. He had not said, No! They do not mean that, they mean something else, let me explain. He had said, Wait! Okay, I said that. But I was right to say that, I was serving my country and my President, it cannot be a crime to say that even if it wasn't exactly true. This was a form of jury nullification, as lawyers call it; you admit you did it, and you say to the jury, Acquit me! Yes I did it, and you'd have done it too, and the law is ridiculous, and I shouldn't be convicted. So ignore that evidence and let me go. And North had done pretty well on it. He had shredded documents by the pound, by the box, and the jury had acquitted him of obstruction of justice. Some people said the judge had almost fallen off the bench when he heard that verdict.

However, North was North, and I wasn't. He was quite a performer. In the end, the jury had convicted him of several counts. Just as Gillen was, I thought, suggesting: they would throw ten or twenty counts at me, the jury would compromise and convict me on only a couple. A couple of felonies.

Rachel called. She had not planned to come this day, Friday, for we had made the decision already, yesterday: Fight! She heard my voice on the phone, and she said, should I come there? Yes. She knew something had happened. What? What had they said to DeVier? I explained. I told her how the lawyers had reacted, how their body language had changed, how obvious it was that they saw this as a very smart move by Walsh and Gillen, much tougher to beat. She was on her way.

She joined us in twenty minutes and was upset before she entered that conference room. The lawyers had done it again. We had made a decision, they had gotten their hands on me, and now there was no decision. Now there was fear, indecision, and faltering.

I tried to explain. I could not really explain, because I was not sure. I had thought, again, stupidly, childishly, innocently, that I understood this game. I had thought they were saying what the congressmen had said: you knew North ran this operation, you knew it was illegal, you knew it all. I had said No, I didn't know. I continued to say no. They were going to try to prove that, and they would never be able to prove it, because it was not so.

But now, now they were changing the rules again. Oh no, we don't have to prove that, they were saying. Yes, we'll tell the jury that, I thought Gillen's new strategy had it, but that's only to sow doubt in their minds. What we have to prove is just this: you said the words, "We didn't have conversations," but North had had conversations. And you knew it. Period.

UNDUE PROCESS

Hmmm. The lawyers were saying, hmmmm. I had said those words. But I asked, wasn't it clear what they meant, then? Hmmmm. You'd have to explain that. Hard to explain those words away. Hard to do jury nullification, adopting the words and defending them, if North had had conversations. This is crazy, this is ridiculous, I said: everyone in the world knew that there had to be some point of contact, some messenger. Was that a crime? No, but that wasn't what you said. You had denied that. Wait, I said, that isn't what I was denying, everyone understood what was being argued about, back then, five years ago. Oh, did they? Would the jury?

And then, balance the weights. Cost-benefit analysis. If you go to trial, and they use this theory, their chances of winning are decent. The jury may say, Hell, he knew something, one count, maybe two, let's compromise, let's get out of here and all be home for dinner. I had served on a jury, right here in the District of Columbia, and I knew that. People kept looking at their watches, balancing the fate of the defendant against the desire to beat the rush hour. The result may be a compromise, and if they do that, you have a felony conviction.

But we might win. There are no guarantees. Barry Levine said, we can fight this, I am ready to fight this, don't give this up and think they have it won. But it depends, too, on what's on the other side. What's the plea? If you have to plead to lying to Congress, that's one thing. If it's one count of a misdemeanor that they invented, that no one ever heard of, this 2 USC 192 stuff, then that's something to think about.

It was clear how they came out. Garment would advise taking the plea. So would Morgan. So would Pierson. But that was very, very personal, they all said, and they wanted to make it clear, crystal clear, that it was my decision, and that if I decided to fight, they were with me all the way, to the end. Levine was different, and he said, look, this is very personal, some people would fight even now, others would not; he did not advise me one way or the other.

Throughout this discussion Rachel was in tears, because she sensed where it was going. This plea bargain was truly the living dead; you could not kill it, it kept coming back and coming back. I asked them all to leave the two of us alone.

Now I really had to decide. This was truly, truly it. No delay, no postponement, no brilliant ideas, no new schemes, nothing. The grand jury would meet the following day. I had to decide. *I* had to do it, right now. In that room. Now.

I knew what Rachel wanted: she wanted to fight. She was geared up, she was ready, she had taken the fighter's crouch, ready for any blows that they rained on us, ready for the whole fifteen rounds, ready even to be knocked down if it came to that. Ready to knock them out, and if we could not do that, at least we would leave them bloodied. They would feel the pain.

For me, that feeling was gone. I wasn't sure why. Maybe the pretrial diversion idea had undone me psychologically, had destroyed the readiness and peace of mind I had felt about the fight, because I had led myself once again to believe there was an escape route. Maybe I had grasped at that straw in the first place because I had never really been ready for the fight. Maybe Walsh's and Gillen's new theory of the case had done it, because for the first time it had shown me how I might lose. It had shown me that they might get a jury to say, Oh well, he must have known something, he must have known North talked to them, he did know North talked to them, so, Guilty! It had changed my picture of the trial. I had thought they were going to have to show I knew something illegal was going on, or knew all about North's operation, and that it was indeed *his* operation, and in my mind I had all the evidence marshaled to disprove that. But now I saw they would only be trying to show some phone calls, some conversations, and I had said, the Government doesn't have conversations with the private network. North had had a telephone, so we might lose the case.

Rachel and I sat there, she in tears. I had never felt so miserable, not since my father's death, as I did at that moment. She said, what do you want to do?

I wanted to disappear. I had never before understood those phrases about wanting to die, wanting to crawl under the ground. How could anyone make this decision? How could you "voluntarily" say, okay, I'm guilty. How could I let those dirty, despicable bastards *win*? How could I let Rachel down? I was silent for a long time. Then I told her, you know what I want to do? I feel like I want to die.

You stop that, she said. Knock that off right now. Right now.

UNDUE PROCESS

Okay. More silence. Finally I told her. I thought it was time to end this. I did not want two more years of it. I did not want this to *be* my life for years more. I wanted it over. I did not want to bankrupt the entire family, and I did not want to take the chance of a felony conviction, disbarment, jail. I would take the plea. There was a way to wake up from this five-year nightmare, and it was to go ahead and do it, to say Yes. I felt I was letting down the side, I felt I should fight, because what Walsh was doing was so wrong, what he stood for was so wrong, this system was so vile and so, well, un-American. But I was tired of holding up the side. I'd done enough of it. I had paid and paid and paid. I had done my part. I could go home now.

I was really scared, though, scared of one thing, I said, one thing only: that she would think I was not the man I had been, not the man taking on all comers, fighting all the good fights. We held each other, and she said, No, no, no, *they* are doing this to us, those fucking animals, those vermin. You are not doing it to us, you are you, and we have to decide how to get through this, and we'll get through it, whatever happens. Whether you fight it and win, or fight it and lose, or don't fight it. Whatever you do and whatever happens, we are a family and we will be together.

She did not agree with my decision. Later a friend told me, if he had refused to do what his wife so deeply believed in doing on a question this important, he was not sure she'd have taken it. I didn't ask him what that implied, but I never for a moment thought I had convinced Rachel. She was not saying, Okay, I agree, you've persuaded me. She was saying, You're my husband, and you have to decide this one, and whatever you decide, that will not change us.

This was the worst day I can ever remember. The decision was literally agonizing, because agony lay in either choice. What if I choose trial and lose, and am sentenced to jail, and have to live with the knowledge that I could have avoided it all, put it all far, far behind me with that plea agreement I so bravely threw away? But if I plead, would I wonder for the rest of my life whether I could have beaten it? Would I dream for years of that sweet moment of victory, of vindication, on the courthouse steps?

Yet as I sat and tried to think, think, think what to do, I had found

the tide pulling me toward a plea agreement. As I try now to reconstruct that day, I cannot do it very well; I cannot remember when I
decided, when the moment came. Perhaps there was no single moment
of decision, only that steady tidal pull toward the plea.

All right. We called the lawyers back, and I said, okay, I have
decided. I will accept the plea.

Now, it's all over, I thought.

Wrong again.

Now there were lots more decisions to make. What are you offer-
ing to plead to? What if they want a cooperation agreement? What
statement can I make in court, or after it? When should this happen?
What about an agreement on the sentence?

Okay. They offered a "minimal" disposition, so that's what it
should be. That means the one misdemeanor count, and under 2 USC
192; not lying, not false testimony, just withholding some information.
For Brunei, because I had five years ago admitted and apologized for
withholding information on Brunei, so there was nothing new here.

Sentence? Community service. No fine, no jail. Under the Federal
Rules of Criminal Procedure, prosecutor and defendant can make a
deal on a sentence, and it binds both of them. The judge cannot change
it. He can reject it, but then the whole plea deal is off. That's what we
want. It's safe and sure.

Cooperation agreement? They can drop dead, I said; tell 'em to
shove their cooperation agreement. I have nothing to tell them. Well,
all the lawyers said, it's standard. You'd have to respond to subpoenas
anyway, so you lose nothing.

Timing? Fast. I'm doing this to get it over with. Let's get it over
with. Let's do it Monday. With an agreement on the quickest possible
sentencing.

All right. Pierson would go back, see Walsh and Gillen, and give
them the news. They'd have a happy day.

Rachel and I went home in separate cars, because we had come
separately. We had to make the calls now: my mother, her parents, my
brother, the other people who needed to be told what would happen
Monday and be in the news that night, and in Tuesday's newspapers.
My mother and my brother were supportive. This sounded like the

right decision. Get It over with. Put it behind you. For Rachel, her parents' reaction was critical, because they, like her, had been ready for the fight. They were great. They said, Right. We are behind you completely. You've done your part. You fought the good fight, you paid your dues, now go ahead and get it all over with.

I had to tell the children. Complicated. Much easier to say, they say I lied, and I didn't, and now there will be a court case. So I said, you know, when I worked in the State Department I had a lot of secrets. And I didn't tell anyone, right? Now, they are saying, the prosecutors are saying, wait a minute, you *had* to tell Congress. It was a crime not to tell them. Do you admit you didn't tell them? And I am saying, well, sure, I admit I didn't tell them. And they are saying, well, that is a crime. And I am saying, well, I don't think so, but if it is, it is. I sure didn't tell, and if that's a crime, that's a crime. They can call it that. I did the right thing in not telling, whatever they say. So now, on Monday, we will go to court, and the judge will ask, did you tell everything you knew to Congress? And I'll say, Nope. And he'll say, well that's a crime. And I'll say, okay, if you say so. And probably they will make me pay a fine, some money, to punish me for not telling.

A lot of money, Sarah asked? More than a thousand dollars? Yes, I said, probably. Well, Daddy, will we go poor? she asked. No, we won't. Nothing will change for you. Everything will be the same. And I thought to myself, boy, I'd like to be nine again. 'Cause if I were nine, I'd actually believe that.

At 9:30 that evening, when the kids were in bed, Pierson called. He had met with Walsh and Gillen. Generally, they accept the plea, he reported, and they accept a sentence of community service, no jail, no fine, and they accept the idea of acting as quickly on sentencing as the judge is willing to move.

But there's one complication. They want a proffer conference with you. What in hell is a proffer conference? I wanted to know. Pierson explained: Well, they describe it as routine. They said with every other plea agreement they have had a proffer conference, so that they can see what they are getting out of this agreement in terms of information. I told them, Pierson said, don't assume you'll get any new information at all. Elliott never said he had a proffer to make. Walsh had answered, Well, we intentionally did not ever ask Elliott about other people's activities. And we only want the truth, that's all. We need to know Elliott's position on various things.

You lying, cheating sons-of-bitches, I thought. First you want a nice gentleman's agreement, you want something "minimal," you like me very much. Now, it's, Who else do you turn in? Now it's, "other people's activities." Levine had been right: you start down this road, and you never know where it leads.

Pierson had said, Wait a minute, I'm not comfortable with this. Where does it lead? What is the effect of it on the plea bargain? What is the effect of what Elliott says, later on? Can it be used against him, or others?

Well, Walsh had replied, if we are not satisfied with his information, not comfortable with how things went, it's all erased. It never happened. Of course, there's no plea bargain, either.

Pierson had asked for an example. What might you ask about? Oh, Gillen had said, here's an example: Noriega. And several times, Pierson told me, they had mentioned Bud McFarlane, for that precedent— the testimony he gave that freed Ollie North—clearly grates on them. They are being more careful now about what people say, and want to have a better grasp of the position people will take. The punchline, Pierson said, is that you have a decision to make: will you do the proffer conference, and if so, what rules do we want? Pierson's own view was that we might as well go ahead with it, because it was hard to see how we were worse off after it than at the start of it.

But we needed to get some other views. That was right, but I fumed, and not at him. Now we were into plea negotiations, and still they wouldn't let me bring in my criminal lawyers.

Time for a conference again, another meeting, and we agreed to meet in Pierson's office the next morning, Saturday morning, at 9 A.M. Because we were scheduled to see Walsh at ten.

SATURDAY, OCTOBER 5

We're Off to See the Wizard

W e met at DeVier's office at 8 A.M. DeVier and me, Barry Levine, Peter Morgan, Len Garment. We had about an hour and a half to figure out where I stood.

Well, Pierson began, they do want a deal. And they do want a scalp. And they also want all the information they can get to help their investigation of others. But let me tell you the whole story, he said.

Pierson had said, Elliott is prepared to plead to a single misdemeanor under 192. And Walsh had said, Oh, no, Oh my, we've never gone below two counts. We need a count on North, knowledge of North's activities, and a count on fundraising, which could be Brunei.

I was stunned. I also felt sick. You are an idiot, I told myself. You are really a moron. You actually thought, even now, even at this point, that they would play fair. You jerk. Now they want two counts. What else do they want? Maybe I won't do it. Maybe they will behave so badly that I *can't* do it. That would be the best: then there's really no choice to make. Maybe they'll save me from this and *make* me fight.

Pierson had replied, I had understood you to be suggesting a disposition on a single misdemeanor count, and that is exactly what I told my client, and that's all the power I have from him, to agree to that.

I believe you, Walsh had said. I believe you believed that. I will need to consult my team on this now.

Oh, your team, I thought. Your wonderful boys. It would be Walsh's "old boy" sense of comity, and the sense he might actually have misled Pierson, versus the pressures the murderers on his staff would bring on the old man. And they had never lost yet.

I am here, Pierson had said, only because of the possibility of an agreement on a single count.

Well, let's agree to leave that an open issue, and move ahead, Walsh had said.

All right, Pierson had said. We'll need a sentence agreement. It should be, no fine, no jail, but community service.

Fine, Walsh had replied, fine. One thousand hours is an impressive number, and will be so to the judge. That will work fine.

Now, in Pierson's conference room, I rebelled. I won't do it, I said. I will not do it. I agreed to that number, I said, when I was not going to be convicted. I was not going to be a criminal.

But I'm not going to do it now. No way. None. That's six months full-time. What am I supposed to live on during those six months? Or if I do it ten hours a week, it will take two years. Two goddamn years. Anybody remember the business about "get this behind you"? That's supposed to be getting it behind me? Forget it. Bud McFarlane, who was National Security Adviser, and in the middle of this, and pleaded to *four* counts, got two hundred hours of community service, and I'm supposed to say, Yeah, okay, give me a thousand.

Fine me. Tell them to fine me. I'll pay it. I'll borrow it, and pay the fine, and pay back the loan when I can. Get them out of my life, I thought. I want these people out of my life. This is slavery. This is serfdom. First Walsh wants to make me a criminal, then he wants me to work off my dishonor for *years*? Aren't they doing enough damage to me and my family already? Can't they at least have the decency to do it and then *go away*? I could see Walsh, pompous, mock-friendly, saying how this would be good for me, help me out, build character. I really needed Lawrence Walsh to help me build my character.

I am not going to do it, I told the lawyers. I am not going to. Period.

They were surprised by my vehemence. I guess I was on that border between rage and tears, but that was all right too: it showed them I meant it.

Now another issue, Pierson had told Walsh, was timing. We want to get it over with, do it all, in one day. Filing, arraignment, and sentencing.

It can't be done in one day if the judge is not ready to sentence, Walsh had replied. But other than that, speed is fine with us.

I need to put something on the table now, very clearly, Pierson had then said. Elliott is very worried about the Alan Fiers precedent on this. Elliott cannot do what Fiers did: he does not have any information about any criminal acts by others. He is not in Fiers's position, and what is more, he doesn't want to be seen to be.

I had insisted that Pierson raise this point. People were angry at Fiers and felt he had turned state's evidence against Clair George. Had turned him in. Had ratted on him. I wasn't doing that, and didn't want people thinking I had.

Hmmmm, Walsh had said. Well, what kind of proffer conference could we have, in that case? Walsh had explained that in any plea bargain we must have a proffer conference. We have to have a proffer conference so that we can fully understand Mr. Abrams's position.

Well, now, wait a minute, Pierson had said. Wait. I thought you were acting in this way in Mr. Abrams's case because, as you had explained it to me, as I understood it, you couldn't *quite* do nothing in this case, couldn't "pass it by," and so instead you were agreeing to, in fact it was you who suggested, a misdemeanor plea. You couldn't do nothing, but you could do this. You were not motivated by proffers.

Oh yes, Walsh had said, sure. But we can't repeat the McFarlane experience again.

They are really spooked by what happened in the North case, I thought, where McFarlane had rescued the prisoner. They had called him, he was a government witness, and on the stand he had freed North. Bravo! I didn't know, or care, whether McFarlane had long planned this revenge against Walsh or had suddenly pounced when, on the stand, he saw his chance. All I knew was that he had screwed

Walsh, which was wonderful. And now Walsh, and Gillen, who had joined the meeting, were nervous.

Gillen had now spoken. If we have a plea agreement, Abrams has to be absolutely candid. In some areas we have not had total candor.

I thought, my gorge rising, you say to these guys, okay, you win, go ahead, make me a criminal. And they are still arguing with you, still pushing their luck. They ask you, what did North say to you on July 8, 1986, and you think, who the hell knows that anyone said to him on July 8, 1986, you moron, but you say, "Mmmm, well, I am not really sure I can recall that, Mr. Gillen." So he says to Pierson, "in some areas we have not had total candor."

Have I had total candor from you, you worthless shit?

Of course, I knew damn well they did not want total candor; they wanted me to remember what was helpful to them. And the truth was, there was a lot I could not remember—including a lot of things that would have helped me. A lot of exculpating evidence. I had repeatedly been amazed at what I had forgotten. I had assumed you forget the stuff that might be considered dangerous, and never forget what helps you out. Wrong. You just plain forget, I had discovered. You forget meetings, memos, calls, even the ones that make you look great. Worse yet, you forget what you knew when. I had tried very hard to remember what I thought North was really up to when I started the job, and how and when I had suspected anything more. And that was impossible to recall, because unless the thoughts, the impressions, were transmitted to someone else in the form of speech or writing, they were long gone.

This much was clear: we were all smart guys, North and Fiers and me, and we had all had the responsibility to be sure neither we nor anyone on our staffs violated the law. And we had tried very hard, or so it had appeared to me. We had spent hour after hour trying to be sure we were not violating the Boland Amendment. Once we had had a long debate over whether we could buy the Contras wristwatches. They had made their request at a time when we were permitted to give them only humanitarian aid—food, shoes, and medicine. Were wristwatches humanitarian aid? Well, how could they be lethal aid? How could you hurt someone with a wristwatch? That was the kind of discussion we had had, in those days in 1986, and I had watched my guys at State and in the embassies, and Alan had watched his guys at the CIA and its stations, and Ollie had watched . . . himself. But we had all known the name of the game, had known the congressional hostility to the Contra program, and were careful. I had thought.

Well, now, Pierson had said to Walsh and Gillen, Elliott will be candid, BUT. What is changing here is one thing only: we now accept responsibility for acts based on *your* bright line distinction. That is, we accept that the testimony that there was absolutely no U.S. Government role went too far. But that's it. Elliott is not changing around his prior testimony.

Now don't get hot, Walsh had said. I foresee no problem here. Don't magnify this out of proportion.

Maybe, I thought, the old gent was worried that Gillen was going too far and would drive me back to fighting this all at trial. Which he might, the way I felt at that point. Two counts. A thousand hours. Proffer conference. What was next? Levine had been right. Levine would take the case. It wasn't too late. They, Walsh and Gillen, didn't want a trial, I knew that. They didn't want to drag this on, didn't want to have to hire more lawyers, didn't want to risk losing. They wanted a nice, clean surrender. And now I was asking, after this battle can the officers keep their horses? And Gillen was saying, walk home. Maybe Walsh realized he was going too far.

What is the result, Pierson had asked, if you ask Elliott things and you are disappointed with the responses? What happens if you don't like his answers? Walsh had replied, that depends on whether we think he has been forthcoming. And, Pierson had said, what if you don't? Well at the worst, Walsh had replied, there's no plea bargain.

I am very uncomfortable about this, Pierson had told them. But it's not an "interview," Walsh had said, there's no FBI agent taking notes for his 302 report; it's just a proffer conference, that's all. If there is no good result, if it doesn't work out, all our discussions are erased. We are not trying to pull away from the agreement with you, but we must have an opportunity to talk to Elliott first.

Let's set a time for tomorrow, Gillen had then said, and let's have the conference. I really don't anticipate any problems, and we can go ahead and file and get this over with on Monday.

I shared Pierson's misgivings. It all sounded like some kind of big trap. Maybe we should junk it all, and go fight them. I was surprised, amazed actually, by Levine's response. Levine was the fighting man, and now he said Oh no, a proffer conference doesn't put *you* at risk, it puts *them* at risk.

What?

Sure, Levine said. *Kastigar.*

Oh, *Kastigar.* What does that mean?

Taint. Boy, he said, you'd think they'd have learned something from the North case, and from McFarlane's freeing North, but I guess not. Look, they'll tell you they will not use anything you say in the proffer conference against you if the plea agreement collapses. They've already told DeVier that: it's all "erased." Okay. Suppose for some reason it all collapses today, or tomorrow, and they indict you. We say, oh no, *Kastigar*! They are using all that proffer conference stuff against you. Taint! Judges hate that kind of stuff. It will help your bargaining position a lot. It will tie them in knots.

So go ahead, he said. Don't worry. Talk freely. Mention anything you like. Just make sure you get in writing that agreement to "erase" it, Levine said. God knows what they'd testify to, what they'd say the agreement was. Right! Now that man thinks like I do, I told myself. He hates them too, he thinks they'll cheat.

Solved. Now that left the sentence issue, and the lawyers explained I might have a problem. The rules of criminal procedure provided for subparagraph "C" sentence agreements, which bind everyone; if the judge doesn't buy it, I can back out of the plea bargain. And they provide for "B" sentence agreements, which bind the prosecutor but not the judge; if the judge doesn't buy it, tough. I'm stuck. There were some other options, too: maybe they would agree not to suggest a particular sentence, just to stand silent at the sentencing. That was possible too, Levine said.

He knew his stuff, I thought, and I was angry again that he was not permitted to come and sit by my side and argue with Walsh and Gillen.

Realize, the lawyers said, that Walsh feels he has something in that thousand hours of community service. If you want to change that, you may have to pay for it. Somehow. Like in the timing of sentencing.

UNDUE PROCESS

That was serious. First, I wanted this over with. That was the whole idea. Plead, finish it, put it behind you. But they had kept Alan Fiers hanging for months without a sentence. This could drag on into 1992. Would you accept that, if that was the price for killing the thousand hours?

Kick me when I'm down, I thought. My tax dollars at work. How could they *do* this? It was so, so *unfair*. So *wrong*. I told the lawyers, maybe. Maybe I'd make that trade. Even if it took a couple of months more that way, it would still end it all faster than with the thousand hours ahead of me.

Okay. Time to go. We're off to see the Wizard, I thought. That was how Rachel and I had come to refer to Walsh, the great unseen power behind the curtain. Now I would see him again, and talk to him, talk to all of them. Now I'd go into their lair, but everything was different now. Because they had won: I was pleading guilty. Sure, the game wasn't exactly over yet, not entirely; Levine had made it clear to me that at any time, at any time, I could still turn around. And there had been moments when I felt like it. But, really, they had won, and I was now going in to see them, not as I had four years before, not as an Assistant Secretary of State backed by the power of incumbency, and not as I had exactly one week before, as a private citizen insisting on his innocence and ready to fight them and beat them, but this time as a man who had agreed to plead guilty. A man who was going to have a "proffer conference" with them, as soon as Pierson and they had negotiated out the remaining "details," like my sentence and the timing of all this.

I drove Pierson over in my car, parked in a lot, and we went upstairs. We had agreed it would be better that I not attend the preliminary negotiating session. It would go better without me there, and go faster as well. Instead, I would wait outside.

"Outside" meant their little reception room, and this day I got to know it well. I spent eight hours there, waiting. Waiting for them to finish, waiting for something to happen, waiting for word from Pierson. On the guard's desk was a telephone, and every hour or two I would call Rachel and say, Not yet. Haven't gone in there yet. Haven't started yet. Have no idea when. Can't imagine. I don't know.

The reading material available was not excellent. I had read the paper that morning, and now I read the guard's copy again. And then again, reading now the classified ads, wondering if I should buy a small dry cleaner's establishment in Northeast or a used Ford truck; reading the high school sports scores, the TV listings, the ads. In England, where I had studied, I would read the Court Calendar in situations like these (well, I thought, not exactly like these), and would see what The Lady Sarah This-And-That had done that day at Balmoral, and that the Ambassador of Sri Lanka had been presented to Her Majesty. No such luck here, so I studied the price of Ford trucks.

Next I read a *Business Week* that was lying around, not realizing it was thirteen months old until I had finished it and looked at the cover. I napped periodically, too, for I had not slept well the night before, or the night before that, or the night before that. Since we left the beach in August, I told myself.

I thought about the kids a lot, and how they did not understand what was happening, and could not, and how in the end I could not really explain it because I did not understand it either. When I was Assistant Secretary of State for Inter-American Affairs, and life for a while had consisted of TV appearances, state dinners, and trips on Air Force planes to see Latin presidents, I used to wonder, When will a safe fall out of someone's window and land on my head? How can anyone be this lucky? All this, and Rachel, and Jacob, and Sarah, and Joey? When will lightning strike me down?

Boom!

I told myself, don't get morbid. This is not tragic. People go through worse. This is shock treatment, this is just being zapped, not fried. And it is, after all, so *interesting*. At least life is still interesting.

I thought about how much I hated those people in there, inside, who had persuaded themselves that the least accommodation with me would wound the Constitution, threaten the Republic. And I used to be accused, the Reagan Administration used to be accused, of being "ideological"!

I thought about what I had done to arouse so deep a hatred on the Left—this undying, undimmed hatred—and I told myself: well, from their point of view, being smart enough to know better, having once (when I had been a Democrat) known better, being better at fighting them than the others in the Administration, and being unrepentant. Was it worth it now? Who could say? This was no big deal: people had died, many, many had died, fighting this Cold War. Now the Cold War is ending, it's over, and no one will ever enjoy the unique opportunity being offered to me right now. Never again will a special prosecutor hound anyone about what he did in those bad old days when fighting Communism was a big issue. This whole process is positively archaic, I thought. Doesn't Walsh read *Newsweek* or watch TV? The Cold War is over. Not even the Russians do political trials any more.

I sat there with nothing to do, and with no way of changing even that. They had me. I was no longer the subject, I was the object. And every passing hour made me feel more helpless, more bored, more anxious about these now endless negotiations. What in hell were they negotiating?

Pierson came out periodically, and he'd report to me, and then I'd report to Rachel. They were actually drafting the documents. The Statement of Facts, the Information (which substitutes for an indictment in a negotiated plea case), and above all the actual Plea Agreement. And there were negotiations on the basic conditions of the plea: They wouldn't give *at all* on the two counts. They wouldn't agree on a sentence other than a thousand hours. They would agree to a fast sentencing, but of course there would have to be a presentencing report, and that takes a couple of months.

The bastards.

Meanwhile morning had turned to noon, and noon to dusk. I went to synagogue with Jacob on Saturday mornings, and in the afternoon we all played ball, rented movies, hung around. Not today. They had killed Saturday, and of course as the day went on it was clear I'd have to come back. They weren't going to start at three o'clock, or four, or five. Come back tomorrow. Kill the whole weekend, don't see the kids at all.

And so it was. After a while Pierson came out, said they had stopped, had done the paperwork, and we'd do the proffer conference tomorrow. Sunday. Okay? Sure, tell them okay. We could still finish up tomorrow, he said, and we are still on for Monday. We will do the filing and the arraignment on Monday. Let's go home.

Perfect day, I thought. I was a slug, sitting on their couch waiting to be salted. And now with the sun going down I would live another day.

I dropped Pierson off, went home, had dinner, and had a normal early evening: baths, stories. Where were you all day, Daddy? Meetings. All day? Yes, and again tomorrow. Oh, Daddy, but we wanted to . . .

Later on Barry Levine called. He had spoken to Pierson, had gotten a report. As always, it was bracing to hear his voice. Here were his thoughts: First, he said, you've got to negotiate that Statement of Facts tomorrow. Along with the information, there would be a Statement of Facts, and it must be limited to the actual count or counts. Don't let them pile it on, he said. Don't let them mention any other "crimes," any other testimony.

Now, as to the counts, he said, one count or two counts, that is not a major obstacle. They want one count on fundraising, meaning not telling Congress about Brunei, and one count on "conversations," on page 11? Don't sweat it. No one will ever remember how many counts there were. It's important that it not be lying or false testimony, important that it just be withholding information, but don't worry about the two counts. This is all such bullshit. You admitted five years ago that you didn't tell Congress about Brunei. You were under strict instructions not to. You were doing your job. And the other count, the "page 11" count, my God, they ought to be embarrassed to put it in writing. There were "conversations"—that's your crime? North was a messenger, North had conversations, and that's what they are going to court with? Any normal U.S. Attorney would be ashamed. No one but these jerks would even bring such a case.

Now, Levine said, as to your proffer conference. Gillen and the boys had prepared a piece of paper for me to sign, and they had mentioned *Kastigar* and shown us they were big boys who knew their stuff. Their piece of paper had said that nothing I said that day could be used as direct evidence against me. Oh well, I thought, that meant our potential advantage if everything broke down, our potential taint argument if things fell apart and we went on to fight them, was gone. What should we do? I asked Levine. Should we fight on this point? Should we fight on their proposed language?

UNDUE PROCESS

Nope, he said. Buy it. They do not understand *Kastigar*. If they think that statement solves their *Kastigar* problem, they are nuts. Take their language, and if things fall apart I will have a terrific time tying them in knots with it.

Now as to the timing of sentencing, he said, we should see if the judge will go ahead without a presentencing report. It's no business of Walsh's; sentencing is the prerogative of the court alone. If the judge will buy it, why not try it? Then, he took me over the relative advantages and disadvantages of "B" and "C" sentence agreements: the advantage of the "C" was certainty, while the advantage of the "B" was that Walsh would not agree to a "C" without the thousand hours. I fumed again. Christ, haven't they heard that the Thirteenth Amendment outlawed slavery?

You have a strong position, Levine said. Tell them you did twelve years of community service. Tell them you did not spend your time making money, you spent it serving your country. Now you want to get on with your life. Put it behind you, they had said; and now they should let you.

The Proffer Conference: Darkness at Noon, Doctors at Twilight

A nother night without sleep, another morning without appetite. We had agreed to meet at 8:30 A.M. in Pierson's office, and this time it was Morgan, Pierson, and me, with Levine on the phone with us.

What were the issues today? The sentence *per se*: what would it be? The timing of the sentence. Whether it's a ''B'' or a ''C'' sentence. Whether the plea agreement should be sealed. The language of the Information and the Statement of Facts. And public statements by me.

I asked what I could say, should say, after arraignment. Well, Levine said, say anything you want *except* don't deny guilt. If you try to run away from it, the judge will be really pissed, and you could pay for that. Accept responsibility for your acts. Say anything you want, really, but remember, until sentencing your future is on the line. Watch it. Better safe than sorry.

What about others, I asked? Rachel. My in-laws. My friends. Well, Levine said, the further away from you, the more freedom they have, the less risk it will be attributed to you, and the less risk it could

145

conceivably hurt you. Rachel should be very careful. Almost as careful as you. Others can say what they want. We still have a First Amendment.

Yeah, I thought; the Sixth is gone, the Thirteenth is gone, but maybe the First is still there. At least for some people, if not for me.

Why do you want to seal the plea agreement, the lawyers asked me? Because I hate it, I said. It sounds like it's about the John Dillinger case, filled with "if you commit further crimes" and stuff like that. I hate it. Relax, they said. No one will read it. Have you ever read the plea agreement in any other case? No, I hadn't. In fact, they said, if you do something unusual, like sealing it, people will say, Why? What are you hiding? Just relax, don't make it an issue. Stick with the real issues: the sentence and its timing.

Okay. Let's go. Time to see the Wizard again. For my "proffer conference." Relax, Gillen had said. Wear blue jeans. No suits, no ties. Just a relaxed conversation.

I felt awful. Tired. Tense. Bewildered. Furious. Sick. Frustrated. Off we went.

Now I understand collaborationism.

Like most Americans my age, I had seen it in books and on the screen: in World War II movies about the French Resistance, in novels about Czarist Russia, in accounts by East European and Soviet citizens about life under the Communist security apparat. It did not seem so complicated or so interesting to me, and it was as foreign to my life in America as accounts of life in outer space.

From the very start of discussions with the prosecutors, I had the clear impression that if I had a sexy enough "proffer," I might avoid prosecution entirely. "Proffer" in this context meant the offer of information that would allow them to indict someone else instead of me—someone else bigger than me. It was very clear that any information about my former boss, Secretary Shultz, or about President Bush or his staff, was top-drawer stuff, the kind of proffer that would set me free. Second-rate information might not get them to turn away from me but would certainly help me in any plea bargain negotiation.

UNDUE PROCESS

The abstract idea was repulsive to me. I had no information of use to the prosecutors, and their belief that I did was of a piece with their general view that I was part of some giant conspiracy that led right into the Oval Office. Beyond this, ratting on someone, even if I had had any information, was repugnant. I had tried very hard to shield the career Foreign Service Officers on my staff from political reprisals by critics of the Administration, and I had succeeded. I was relieved that the public criticism, and the possible prosecution, were focused on me, not on people who had worked for me.

I was repelled not only by the idea that I would be asked to ruin the life of a former colleague but by the odd Communist Chinese quality of the process. This was not only prosecution but "reeducation" as well. You were to admit your political errors, denounce all former colleagues, renounce your former political beliefs, and join the other side. It was not simply a matter of admitting the commission of an act or acts that went beyond the bounds; that was only the beginning. As Lenin said, he who says A must say B, and they wanted that too: tell us who else shared your moral degeneracy, who else believed what you believed, who your friends were, whom you talked to. At times it seemed to me I could solve my problems if I would announce I were ready to reregister as a Democrat and admit my political errors. Revolting stuff. I told myself it was not only that I had no information of use to them, but also that I had a moral objection to this conduct by prosecutors in a highly political case.

I had nothing to hide, could not incriminate anyone, did not see any risk. So I wore my blue jeans, and on that Sunday morning, after that last meeting with my lawyers at DeVier Pierson's office, set out for Walsh's lair.

As I drove out of the garage in Pierson's office building, a gigantic 1978 Chrysler New Yorker backed into my car. There was a twenty-minute delay as I inspected the damage and exchanged licenses and insurance information with the other driver. She turned out to be a Dutch girl visiting the United States as a tourist, and her insurance had been taken out by her brother in Colorado; he listed his job as "unemployed" and his telephone number as "none." Not the best start for the day. Pierson called ahead to tell Walsh we'd be late, and came back to tell me how he had resisted temptation: "I had a strong urge to tell him, look, we've had an accident. I'm all right, but Mr. Abrams is dead."

No such luck. We arrived about 10:15 A.M. We returned to the small conference room where Walsh and his staff meet with "outsiders." It is about 12' by 14', crammed with a large table and too many chairs, all hideous government issue. The proffer conference began.

In the next two hours, I was to experience a revulsion, at times a self-revulsion, so great that it would produce physical illness and send me to a hospital emergency room later that day. For I learned that collaborationism was possible, was possible in America, was possible for me. I tasted the temptation to burn my friends to save myself. I realized that the more I hurt others, the more I helped myself; and I wanted, for a moment, to do it. The feeling was literally sickening.

They did not begin with the hard core, for they are not stupid. They began with easy questions about my old job, the paper flow, the information flow. Who talked to whom? Who handled what? Who and who were friends? It was easy, like chatting with people who show a wholesome, friendly interest in your work. No tricks, just straightforward questions. What was the Deputy Secretary's role? What was the Under Secretary's? Where did cables come in? Who got copies? They were like graduate students, fascinated and respectful. Explain to us the wondrous deeds you used to do—please.

Then they began to introduce contradictions between what I was saying and the accounts others had offered, or at least ones they were saying others had offered. Their references to others were couched in a quiet negative, as if to say, "we want to believe you, we do believe you, but we must somehow deal with John Doe's account. Help us." They were interviewing me as an expert witness, as a friend, not a defendant, not an enemy. Want some more coffee? Need a break? It was collegial. The only problem is these others, you see. What shall we make of their stories? Help us. Surely they are wrong, but we need to see how. How did it work?

And I found myself helping. No big deal. It's only process, at first. No, you see, X didn't like Y, A didn't report to B. Let me explain. Process, plus a bit of personality. Office politics. Nothing serious. They must know it all already anyway, right? Then there are those contradictions It's fair to help explain them, isn't it? Some other people may have gotten things wrong. I'm just setting the facts straight. Who attended that meeting. What the date of the decision was. Facts. No criticism of anyone. Not really helping them, right? Just the facts, ma'am, as Sergeant Friday used to say. And they are so serious, so interested, these graduate students. It was no accident that Gillen let a young, fresh-faced assistant of his take the lead.

It is not a slippery slope, it is a trap door, and once you are over it you begin to fall. And I did not even notice it as my velocity increased. I was totally unaware of the "Stockholm Syndrome" taking hold of me, but as the minutes passed the State Department began to lose any reality as a place. The only real place was that room, the only real people were those people, smiling at me, sitting across from me. They were my friends, they wanted to help me. There were, somewhere else, people who wanted to harm me, call me a criminal, but these friendly young men could stop that. They could call it off. They had power over me and they were smiling at me. If I could only help them. State was so far away, so long ago; who really knew who was a friend and who was not? These were my friends. They only wanted to know what really happened, they said. How could that be wrong? And there were people who had misled me, and maybe were lying about me, bad people, back at State, so far away; couldn't I help identify them? Couldn't I explain why they were bad, and lying? Then these good people could help me. If I could help them. Of course. Yes. They had power, they would help me.

And suddenly there is nothing underneath you, it is a freefall, and you must reach up and grasp the hands being stretched out to you, the hands across the table. You want to. You need to. So you begin to search your mind: A was probably not such a good guy. B really liked him better than he liked me. C and D kept secrets from me. Maybe, anyway, so why not mention it? It could be true, couldn't it? I have no power, I can't get people in trouble, I only have to help my friends here, nothing outside the room matters, the past is dead, why does it matter? The future matters, and my friends will protect the future. They will use their power. Didn't C once say he had met D? Perhaps? I should tell my friends.

UNDUE PROCESS

You search your mind, because the operating principle is crystal clear: the worse, the better. The more people you can hurt, the worse you can hurt them, the more doubts you can sew, the more names you can mention—why, the better citizen you are, the more you are helping Justice.

This does not take place in an hour. It takes place in minutes, and finally that moment comes when you are searching for more to say, digging for more to say, in a kind of panic, and then, then, you are at the bottom of the pit. And at the bottom, I woke up. I cannot tell why; I do not know. But I looked across and suddenly I did not see friends, I saw the men who really were sitting there, prosecutors trying to invert every value I had ever been taught to respect. In the interests of Justice, I was being asked to ruin the lives of friends and colleagues, to rat on men who had risked their lives for their country time after time, to join the witch hunt—to save myself. To become an informer, which was the highest honor Walsh had to offer, and be rewarded with a free pass. At the slight cost of a lifetime of self-revulsion.

In those minutes I came to understand collaborationism, and the heart of it does not come through to the collaborator as fear; it comes through as security. The world has become a fearful place before you enter the room, and in that room you are offered safety; indeed it is made clear that in all the world you can find safety only in that room, only with those people. The reeducation part of it is as much self-generated as imposed, in the end, for it is necessary to excuse yourself, above all to yourself. Reeducation may be welcome as a moral escape tunnel, for with the new values will come approval for what you have done. Indeed, you can be a new man, as the Communists always saw; the new man who has shrugged off the old bourgeois ties of friends, colleagues, loyalties, except to the Party. And since he is loyal to the Party, he is a good man.

Arthur Koestler, meet Judge Walsh.

The "proffer conference" ended, and Pierson and I went downstairs for lunch at a nearby McDonalds. Nothing big had happened, we thought. They must have seen I had no useful information, but they had no right to be surprised. We had told them so from day one.

We went back upstairs, and I sat outside in the waiting room again for a few hours, while Pierson negotiated with them on the paperwork. They had come back in, he later told me, and had told him that though they had gotten nothing out of the proffer, they were willing to proceed anyway.

So it would be tomorrow. Monday. I called Rachel, told her it was on, and she then called her mother to ask her to come down to Washington and stay with us. She could help with the kids, pick them up at school at three, and answer phones we did not wish to answer.

And I sat there. It was really going to happen. Tomorrow.

I was called in to look at the documents. We settled the sentence business. They would come off the thousand hours, but not very far. That was just too much for Walsh to grant me. Too much for him. He had gotten the plea, was making me a criminal, had his two counts, had it *all*, but he had to have more.

The good-cop, bad-cop routine he and Gillen had played had worked, briefly. But the man I had once thought might be reasonable, might even be fair, could not bring himself that far. He had it all, and he had to have his hundreds and hundreds of hours too.

Walsh told us, the judge won't impose that stiff a sentence; why not just rely on the court? I talked it over with Pierson, and with Levine and Morgan by phone, and decided to do just that: I would rely on a real judge, not Judge Walsh.

It is bizarre, I thought. He actually admits his proposal is excessive, no court would ever impose it, but he won't back off. Oh he will, he'll take some hours off, Pierson told me; the thousand is not written in concrete. But the court is likely to be fairer. I agreed, and agreed there should be no sentence agreement at all. Nothing. I would just take the risks and hope for the best. We'd ask the judge to set a sentence date as fast as possible. Walsh agreed to that and agreed that he wouldn't speak to any particular sentence. He'd stand mute. Mute Mr. Gillen, it would be.

Now they left us to ourselves so that Pierson could start working on the papers, editing the Statement of Facts, the Plea Agreement, and the Information. I could barely keep my eyes open. I was dead tired, exhausted, washed out. Empty. I decided, why try to stay awake? I nodded off once again, then again.

Pop! Someone had thrown a ball at my chest. Not a hardball, not a softball, maybe a whiffle ball. Pop! I sat up, shaken, startled awake. I'd been sleeping, maybe it was a dream. Maybe someone had thrown something. No, that was out, Pierson was working away. A dream, probably. Or maybe just a small heart attack.

Maybe. My father had had a massive coronary at age forty-five, and I was forty-three. He had been under great stress, I reminded myself, but that could hardly comfort me.

I had once before believed I was having a heart attack. I had gone down to Honduras to visit the Contra camps. I was not well; I had just come back from Haiti, where I had picked up an intestinal parasite, later diagnosed as schigella. For a week I had been living on toast and tea. In Honduras, on the flight back from the camps to Tegucigalpa, I had begun sweating profusely, feeling dreadfully sick, wanting to vomit. I had fallen asleep, fainted really.

When we landed I had gone to try to rest at the Ambassador's residence, but my left arm had begun to tingle. I knew what that meant: heart attack. Death. At forty. I had felt my left arm and hand tingling, and my heart beating too fast, and had thought, Jesus Christ, I am going to die. In Honduras. In Tegucigalpa, Honduras. How will they even get the body back? What a place to die. ''Elliott Abrams Dead at 40 in Banana Republic.'' But it had turned out to be dehydration, and a course of antibiotics for the parasite and rehydration for me had taken care of it.

Now, I was feeling the tingle again, and I knew I was not dehydrated. So I started being scared.

What about my pulse? I clocked it. It was 125. That's too high, I thought. Whatever normal is, that's not it. And I felt awful. And I had felt that Pop! Right in my chest.

My father had been so, so lucky: he had had his coronary *in* a hospital, where he had rushed to visit a sick relative. Maybe this was not a heart attack. Maybe the heart attack would come in a minute. Or an hour. I felt worse. My heart was pounding, I was scared. And why sit there? Have the heart attack in the hospital, I thought. Save your life. No, don't make a big deal. It's probably nothing. Just need a guy to check it out. Right here.

DeVier, I said, I'm sorry to tell you this, but I don't feel very well. Alarmed, he asked what was the matter and said, Do you want to be checked out? Yes. He went to tell the Wizard, who, he later told me, had turned pale. No surprise. This affair had driven Bud McFarlane to a suicide attempt; were they going to have another casualty here? I almost smiled at the thought.

We decided—Pierson decided—that it would be best to run down to the emergency room at George Washington University Hospital. Okay. Walsh's car would take me, Pierson said, and I smiled. I hadn't known he had a car. Nice deal, being Independent Counsel. Maybe I should die in his car, I thought. "Abrams Dead in Walsh Limo." Terrific headline. How about a subhead, "Foul Play Suspected."

We drove off, Pierson and the chauffeur in the front, me lying on the back seat, staring at the roof.

I wonder if I will die, I thought. I wonder if the doctor will say, Sir, you are having a heart attack. Will they go ahead and prosecute a guy who has just had a heart attack? Or is that supposed to be something the judge takes into account at sentencing, that they have destroyed not only your career, but your health, too.

This gave me some sick satisfaction, at first, for a moment. This will shatter Walsh, I thought; I'll beat him, I'll die! Hah! Then I thought, maybe, maybe I will never see my kids again. Maybe I will die right in this car, and I will never see them again. Never. I will never even be able to say goodbye to them and to Rachel and to my mother. My mother will not survive this. My kids, will my kids forget me? Will Joey forget me? He's only six now. What will he remember in five years? Five years, just the time this wretched scandal has taken, it's almost his whole life. Will I ever see them again? Will they have to see me in a hospital bed, with tubes sticking into me, looking like a monster?

We reached GW, I walked into the emergency room, and they asked me, Are you experiencing any pain? No. Not now. They put me into a little room. Oxygen tubes in my nose. Heart monitor on my chest.

I remembered the heart monitors. My father had had one. Each time he had moved, his heartbeat had increased and I had practically fainted watching the blips go up, higher, higher, on the screen. Now I had one. I lay there. They took an EKG, read it, and questioned me some more. Are you under stress and pressure, the doctor asked? Uh, Yes. Is it family, or job-related? Oh, it's job-related, I said. Ah, are your losing your job, she asked. No, that's not exactly my problem, I said.

After a while more doctors and nurses came. How do you feel? Better. Your heart rate is going down. Good. Stay here for a while. Okay.

The resident on duty came and told me, you seem okay. I see no damage to the heart. I don't think it was a heart attack. It seems to be this pressure you are under. Yes, I said, lots of tension these past weeks. Okay, he said, wait a while, lie here, and if it all checks out we won't keep you. Go see your own doctor this week. I'll call him now and tell him you are here. Okay.

He left, and I lay there watching them all work. It was now about 4:30 or so. They are kids, I thought, all these doctors and nurses are kids. I have ten years on them. No, fifteen. I am forty-three and I have a heart problem. No, I have no heart problem, I have a Walsh problem. No *deus ex machina* ending here, I have to go back.

At five they let me go, and Pierson and I raced off for the Wizard's lair. Wow, the resident later told my doctor, I've seen guys wired, but your patient Abrams took the cake. Wow! I stopped for a minute to call Rachel, and I lied to her. I did not tell her I was calling from the GW emergency room. I said, look, this is dragging on. We'll finish tonight, but go ahead and give the kids dinner. And yes, we are still on for tomorrow.

We returned to Walsh's office, and they were all so solicitous. How are you? Good to see you. Are you okay? We were really worried.

I felt weak, but not too weak to feel I would like to spit on all of them. Oh spare me your concern, I wanted to say, spare me your display of humanity, spare me your How are yous. Almost lost your boy, huh? Almost got cheated again. What a scandal. First you lose the

UNDUE PROCESS

North case, then you kill Abrams. Merciless!, the editorials will say, Horrifying! Enough! You know, you wouldn't survive, you bastards. The ultimate sacrifice! If I just died right now, you'd be out of business. It's almost worth it, I thought to myself.

I called Rachel again, told her I had been at GW, but now I am okay. She was horrified I hadn't told her, but relieved that I sounded okay. I felt like shit; I sounded okay because I was getting that Oscar for these weeks of sounding okay on the telephone. I was earning it the hard way.

They called me back in. We were almost done. The Information and Statement of Facts were done, and they were okay. Change this and that, and we were done. Everyone was so happy to see me alive, breathing, pleading, losing, capitulating. They were all so kind. Just sign here.

We discussed the changes Pierson and I wanted. Walsh was hurrying through it now. He wanted it over. Maybe he thought I would die before I signed. Maybe he didn't want me dying right there in his office: oh, the scandal of it. But if I had to die, I wanted to die right there. I want to die in his arms, I thought to myself. Goodbye, Judge, I would say. Always remember, YOU DID THIS TO ME. He wanted me to go home. Okay, he said; all right; just tell us all you've got. Okay. Hmmm. Hmmmm. We can fix that. All right. We agreed fast on the language changes. We agreed on the schedule for tomorrow.

Time to sign the plea agreement.

I signed.

I went home.

One more time, we explained it to the kids. We watched TV. We went to bed.

MONDAY, OCTOBER 7

The Arraignment

O n Monday we had a normal breakfast, then Rachel took the
kids to school and came home. Pierson called at 9:30. The
arraignment is at two, he said, with Judge Robinson. I'll send
a car for you at 12:30, then pick me up, and we'll get there early. Is
your statement done?

We had the morning free, and we watched TV. Oh, there was a lot
to watch those days.

There were the Gates hearings. I loved watching the Gates hearings. A senator later called me to tell me that one morning he had
turned on his radio and heard ". . . accused of telling Congress much
less than he really knew about the Iran/Contra affair." And he had
thought, damn, they are going after Elliott again, trying to prosecute
him on criminal charges for that testimony. Then he had heard ". . .
but Gates will probably be confirmed, experts say, as Director of
Central Intelligence."

It was ludicrous. I watched Gates, I rooted for Gates, I listened to
the jerks on the committee question him. I *was* Gates. It was the same
"offense": You knew more than you told. Of course he did. And now

he would be DCI and I would be a criminal. It did not make me angry, because these kinds of things, I told myself, don't happen in *America*; they only happen in Washington. Isn't justice when two similarly situated people are treated similarly? Rachel and I sat and watched the Gates hearings as if we were observers from the moon.

Then there was Thomas. The juicy hearings were starting that very day, Monday, and I was amazed to find myself thinking, here is a man who has it worse than I do. Think of it, a man who is having a worse day than I am, and I am pleading guilty today. I am a criminal today, and I feel sorry for this man. Suzanne Garment, Len's wife, had said to me, the prosecutors can abuse you, and hurt you, and indict you, but they have lost the power to stigmatize. I liked that, and I agreed with it. But Thomas was being stigmatized, and I felt sorry for him.

And I felt, only, only, only in Washington. Was there anywhere else in America this could possibly happen? I felt this as another bond with Thomas. And then he said something that hit me right in the heart: He said to those Senators who had countenanced and delivered to the TV this disgusting assault on his character and his life, Senators, I grew up thinking that if you just did your best, things would come out right in the end. And you have robbed me of that faith.

That was it. I did not think this could happen in America. Now it was happening. But I wanted to call Thomas and say, you know, it doesn't happen in America. Only here, in this cesspool. Welcome to Your Nation's Capital.

There were a few cars of photographers waiting outside the house, sharks coming to feed, and Rachel and I made sure not to show ourselves at the window. The doorbell rang, one of them had actually had the nerve to ring the doorbell. Rachel yelled at him and he went away. The doorbell rang again, and my mother-in-law said, I'll go, you stay here. Another one, I thought; how many will there be? A minute later she was back with a pamphlet in her hand. Who was it? A Jehovah's Witness canvassing the neighborhood. Divine sense of timing, I thought.

The car came, and off we went. When we arrived at the Court-house the TV cameras and still photographers were already gathered on the steps. This was like old times, like testifying in the old days. I

walked through them, waved at a few familiar faces, told them, Noth
ing now; I'll have something on the way out.

John Barrett, one of Gillen's assistants, greeted us, and we shook
hands. I did not introduce Rachel, but Pierson did, courteous to a fault.
How do you do, Barrett said, sticking out his hand; but Rachel looked
him in the eyes and refused to allow that courtesy, that gesture of
civility, that touch, to these people. Barrett paled and walked on. We
met the others, including Gillen, and Rachel refused to speak to any of
them, or shake hands. They appeared surprised. I mean, indicting
someone is okay, twisting lives is okay, being despicable, politically
motivated, careerist bastards is one thing, but this woman would not
shake hands! Terrible!

We waited in some abandoned judges' chambers, and I signed the
rest of the papers. I felt fine. I had read in the papers that at his
arraignment Clair George had looked pale. Not me, I thought. I want
to look great. Arrogant. Self-possessed. I was absolutely determined
not to give them the victory of making me look bowed, beaten. Never,
I had told myself, and I found I could do it. This wasn't so hard. The
decisions had been hard, the waiting had been hard, but this, this was
easy.

They called us down at five before two, and we found that the
courtroom was full of reporters, the jury box full of sketchers, waiting
to draw me. Rachel sat in the first row. I said to myself, be relaxed.
Look composed at all times, every second. Lean back. Cross your
legs. Look bored. Smile at someone.

The Judge entered the courtroom, the Honorable Aubrey Robinson, Chief Judge of the U.S. District Court for District of Columbia,
and the proceedings began: All rise, this honorable court, all that stuff.
The Judge had just called on Gillen to speak when, suddenly, Ring!
Bing! Bells were sounding, and no one knew what to do. The clerk was
sent to investigate, and a second later he returned and said, Fire Drill!
Everyone Out! Out of the building!

Robinson sneaked out the door behind the bench, and we headed
for the main doors, where we had entered. There was a big crush. I
turned to Gillen, pointing my finger, and said, "Don't blame me!" He
and his crowd laughed, and the reporters took note. Some later wrote,

"A relaxed Abrams even joked with the prosecutors." No Clair George pallor here.

We walked downstairs, milled around, took refuge in our car, drove around for ten minutes. Then we went back, and a guard let us in at the front of the line. At 2:30 it began again. For real this time. Here is how it went:

PROCEEDINGS

THE CLERK: Criminal Case No. 91-575, the United States vs. Elliott Abrams. For the government, Mr. Gillen; for defendant, Mr. Pierson.

THE COURT: Mr. Pierson.

MR. PIERSON: Good afternoon, Your Honor, I'm Devier Pierson, I'm appearing on behalf of the defendant, Elliott Abrams in connection with this brief misdemeanor plea. I think Mr. Gillen has some papers to hand up to the Court.

MR. GILLEN: Your Honor, as the Court is aware, we have filed a two-count information 90-1-0575, the Court has the file on that. We also have the original of the waiver of Section 194 and the original of the plea agreement that the Court has seen to be a courtesy copy. If I could tend that now, Your Honor?

THE COURT: Let's hold on a minute and see if we've got to get out of here.

First things first.

(Fire Drill.)

(Off the record.)

THE COURT: Things thinned out after the fire drill, didn't it? Well, you were rudely interrupted, you may proceed.

MR. GILLEN: Thank you, Your Honor. As I was stating to the Court, the original information has been filed, courtesy copies have been sent to the court and to opposing counsel.

At this time, I'd like to tender the original plea negotiation as well as the waiver under Section 194 to the Court.

(Pause.)

THE COURT: All right, Counsel, will you and Mr. Abrams come forward, please?

You're Elliott Abrams, is that correct?

MR. ABRAMS: That's correct.

THE COURT: And I understand that you are tendering a plea to information which charges you with two counts of violation of Title 2 of the United States Code, Section 192, is that correct?

MR. ABRAMS: Correct.

THE COURT: Have you read and discussed with Mr. Pierson in detail the information that's filed in this case?

MR. ABRAMS: Yes, I have, Your Honor.

THE COURT: And have you discussed with Mr. Pierson in detail the plea, the written plea agreement that has been entered into between you, counsel, and independent counsel?

MR. ABRAMS: Yes, I have.

THE COURT: I am required by law to advise you that if I accept your plea of guilty to the two counts charged in this information, but with respect to each count, there is a maximum penalty of one year imprisonment and not more than $100,000 fine and I must assess a $25 special assessment and that is with respect to each count and with respect to the minimum of the statute that there is a minimum imprisonment of 30 days with a minimum fine of not less than $100 and again the special assessment.

Has that been discussed with you and do you understand that?

MR. ABRAMS: Yes, Your Honor.

THE COURT: And do you understand further that under the terms of the plea agreement that the sentence in this matter will be determined solely by the Court?

MR. ABRAMS: Yes, I do.

THE COURT: Within these limitations that I've stated?

MR. ABRAMS: Yes, sir.

THE COURT: I'm also required to tell you that you have a right to go to trial on each count of this information, to have the assistance of counsel, the government can be required to produce its evidence and convince a jury beyond a reasonable doubt of your guilt or the case may be tried to the Court if you waive the jury trial and the waiver is accepted by the Court.

You have a right to present evidence in defense of the charges and you have a right to the issuance of process for any witnesses that you would desire. But if I accept your plea of guilty to these two counts of the information, do you understand you will have waived those rights to trial?

MR. ABRAMS: I understand that, Your Honor.

THE COURT: All right, very well.

Count 1 of the information charges that on October the 10th, 1986, you were testifying before the Senate Committee on Foreign Relations and in so testifying failed to testify fully with regard to the nature and extent of the contacts between the United States Government and people supplying the so-called Contras.

Count 2 of the information charges that in testifying before the permanent Select Committee of the House on Intelligence that you defaulted and refused to fully answer with respect to foreign governments that were helping to supply the Contras.

That, in essence, are the—these are the charges that are set forth in the information. Do you understand those charges?

MR. ABRAMS: I do, Your Honor.

THE COURT: With respect to Count 1 of the information, how do you plead?

MR. ABRAMS: I plead guilty.

THE COURT: With respect to Count 2 of the information, how do you plead?

MR. ABRAMS: I plead guilty.

THE COURT: Is there anything that the independent counsel would like to relate to the Court before I accept these pleas?

MR. GILLEN: Your Honor, we would tender to the Court a written statement of facts for the factual basis for the guilty plea.

THE COURT: Do you want to summarize those facts any more than I have summarized them?

MR. GILLEN: Just very briefly, Your Honor. I don't believe it's necessary to read the document.

THE COURT: No, it isn't, that's why the law gives us the opportunity to summarize them.

MR. GILLEN: I have gone over this with opposing counsel, the written statement of facts, and there's an agreement as to those facts. Essentially as to Count 1, Your Honor, Mr. Abrams was aware that Colonel North had in fact been a principal channel of communications within the United States Government to the private benefactors and that he had had conversations with them and that he had encouraged them in their endeavors to support the Contras. He withheld this information from Congress on October the 10th.

In Count 2, briefly summarizing Count 2, the evidence would show that when asked if any other foreign governments were helping the contras that Mr. Abrams was aware that the Sultan of Brunei had promised $10 million and that at the time Mr. Abrams made that statement on October the 14th for HPSCI, that he expected that that money would be provided.

That's the summary, Your Honor, of the factual basis.

THE COURT: Do you have any representations to make with respect to that summary, Mr. Pierson?

MR. PIERSON: No, Your Honor, we have reviewed the summary that has been filed with the Court and understand that to be the basis of the government's charge to which Mr. Abrams has made his plea.

THE COURT: And do you know of any reason why the Court should not accept Mr. Abrams' plea to the two counts of this information?

MR. PIERSON: I do not.

THE COURT: All right, I will accept the plea of guilty to each of the counts of the information.

Now, under the plea agreement, as the Court understands it, there are matters, unfinished matters as between Mr. Abrams and the Office of Independent Counsel, is that correct?

MR. GILLEN: That is correct, Your Honor. The agreement provides for Mr. Abrams to assist us and to cooperate in our investigation. It also provides for both the defense and the government today to ask the Court to set down a date certain for his sentence and that we would not ask for a continuance on that matter.

THE COURT: Well, Mr. Pierson, what is your request with respect to a day certain as to sentencing?

MR. PIERSON: Your Honor, we would like the earliest date certain that accommodates the necessary pre-sentencing procedures and Your Honor's schedule.

THE COURT: All right.

(Pause.)

Would you want that this month?

MR. PIERSON: We would like that within a month to six weeks.

THE COURT: Well, I'd rather not have to request an expedited report from the Probation Office and I routinely get those reports till they complete the file and so that I can exercise my judgment with respect to sentencing. Those ordinarily take about a month.

MR. PIERSON: About a month?

THE COURT: Yes. So that why don't I set the sentencing date for—what about the 15th of November?

MR. PIERSON: That is fine.

MR. GILLEN: Fine, Your Honor.

THE COURT: Is that acceptable?

MR. PIERSON: Yes, it is.

THE COURT: That's subject to whatever adjustment counsel and the Court want to make, it's not a—that's a target date for us and we'll set it for 10 o'clock in the morning on the 15th.

MR. PIERSON: Thank you, Your Honor.

THE COURT: Meanwhile, Mr. Abrams is on his personal recognizance. I will, however, Mr. Pierson, ask you to take Mr. Abrams to the appropriate person in the Probation Office so we can start that procedure and if you do that today, we'll expedite it and we'll have everything in place on the 15th.

MR. PIERSON: Thank you, Your Honor.

MR. GILLEN: Thank you, Your Honor.

THE COURT: All right, anything further from counsel?

MR. GILLEN: No, Your Honor.

THE COURT: Will you file these, please?

(Pause.)

All right, we can stand in recess.

(Whereupon, at 2:40 P.M., the hearing was concluded.)

I thought, as we finished, the judge has made a big mistake: He never swore me in! He probably forgot, what with the fire drill business. What does it mean? Am I free? Can I now say, Hah! Just fooling! I had my fingers crossed!

You don't go home after the arraignment, you go to see your probation officer.

I was numb. I had been numb in the courtroom, freezing out all emotions, not feeling, just calculating: this is how I want to look. I did not feel anything at all about this probation stuff. I did not feel humiliation, sorrow, anger, *anything*. I met the officer, a man about fifty, and he gave me forms to fill out. We shook hands and made an appointment for a couple of days later.

Now it was time to go outside and meet the press, down on the steps. There was a big semicircle of them, and I went into the middle. I read my statement:

UNDUE PROCESS

I have today pleaded guilty to violating 2 USC 192 by withholding information from Congress on two occasions during the testimony I gave in 1986. The information withheld related to activities of the United States Government regarding Central America which at that time I believed to be proper and lawful.

I take full responsibility for my actions and for my failure to make full disclosure to Congress in 1986.

I am proud to have given twelve years serving the United States Government and proud of the contribution I made in those years, and very happy to have this entire matter—at long last—behind me.

The press guys didn't like it. I walked away quickly, but I could hear the reactions. Elliott, did you lie to Congress? Don't you feel repentant at all, Elliott? Is that all you are going to say? Won't you apologize?

Screw all of you, too, I thought to myself. You go apologize. Apologize to Jim Wright? To the guys who spent their time plotting with the Communists against their own government? You can all drop dead. I was glad they hadn't liked the statement, because that meant they were seeing me as I wanted them to see me. Tough. Unbowed. Unhurt by Lawrence Walsh and his vicious little team. And the more I thought about that, the more I felt that way. I had done it, I thought, and I had gotten through it. It was over. I was alive. I was fine. I had survived. Rachel was by my side. They had gotten me, but they had not beaten me. You were hit, a friend said later, but it's just a flesh wound. I would sleep fine that night. Finally.

Gee, Officer Krupke

As expected, the plea was big news. It hit the TV news on Monday night, and on Tuesday was on the front page of most papers, including the *New York Times* and *Washington Post*. Most of the stories were only half right; I can barely recall any event I have known a lot about that the press has gotten 100 percent right. The *New York Times* was the best, because its reporter had tried hard, had talked to the lawyers, and knew what questions to ask. The radio and TV reports were the worst, getting the basic facts wrong, saying, "Abrams pleaded guilty to perjury," or "Abrams pleaded guilty to lying to Congress."

But I didn't much care, and the flash of anger was only that: a flash. It was more important to see how this affected my mother and my children.

My mother was okay, for a reason I had not predicted. People were calling her up, not just her friends or relatives, but casual acquaintances, to say, What a travesty! What an outrage! Those S.O.B.s in Washington! As she tried to work out in her own mind how to react to the whole horrible mess, these calls and conversations became important: they told her that others, people who were outsiders, felt what she did, felt that her son had been wronged by a rotten system. On the phone she sounded better.

For the children, it was harder. They heard the TV reports; we did not try to stop that. They, or at least Jacob, the oldest, saw the newspaper. There was one thing I wanted to keep from them. I did not want them to hear the word "jail." Each time the TV reports came to that point, as the reporter was saying "And Abrams could face—" I would hit the MUTE button. When they did hear the word, by accident, I said to them, boy, those stupid reporters make me mad, saying that. Why don't they find out the true facts?

It was a bet with fate, with very, very large stakes. If it turned out I had been betting right, and the sentence was as light as McFarlane's had been, I was doing the right thing in keeping them from worrying about jail. If I were wrong, and there was jail time, I would be doubling the damage by denying the possibility so strongly in advance. I placed the bet.

But you cannot protect them from everything. Rachel picked Sarah up the next day at school and immediately noticed something was wrong. What had happened? Sarah began to cry, explaining that one of her classmates had gone around telling the others, "Did you hear about Sarah's Dad? He's going to jail."

It did not break my heart to hear that story. It was too much for me, and I froze it out; I froze up instantly and did not let myself feel anything. Rachel took charge, talking Sarah through it, calling the other girl's mother to ask that she talk with her child. The woman was mortified, and she did talk with her daughter, and the incident was not repeated. It turned out that this girl's father had died, at a young age, the year before, and one could see in an instant how she had reacted to the news that something bad was going to happen now to someone else's Dad. Which was a good reminder to us all to keep everything in scale.

Incidents like this do not leave a child's mind, and the kids showed a degree of irritability and a lack of concentration that clearly reflected the tension in the air, the mysterious sense that something was wrong, something bad was happening, and it was not over yet. I could not figure out what to do. I tried to be cheerful with them. I tried to resume the most normal schedule possible. I tried to find chances to talk about next summer—which camp they would go to, what house we should rent at the shore in Delaware—to show them that life was going to be normal.

For Rachel, these were days of rage, pent-up, inexpressible, murderous rage at the prosecutors. For what could she *do*? How could she show it, reflect it, get rid of it? How could she help me, not in the emotional or psychological sense, but the real world, what-is-the-next-step-in-the-process sense? People say, Oh it is harder on your wife, and *it is,* and I think that's the reason: you have things to do, you are busy, while she is left to brood.

For I was, somewhat to my surprise, busy, in fact very busy. It turns out that being a criminal takes up a lot of your time.

First of all, letters and phone calls were starting to come in. From old friends. Former colleagues at State. People I had once addressed in some speech or met at some dinner. College roommates. Relatives. Answering all of them was taking hours and hours, day after day.

Then, of course, the lawyers were helping. We had arrived at discussions of the next phase, sentencing. What will the probation officer want? What things should I say and not say? What about people who say they want to write to the judge about sentencing? And the letter to the judge from my lawyers, really a legal brief setting forth our stand on the facts, the law, the appropriate sentence. I spent many hours working on that with them, drafting sections of it, rereading, again, the testimony I had given in 1986. Days go by fast, and there is no time to mope.

Probation officer. Every time I heard the phrase, I could not stop myself from thinking of "Gee, Officer Krupke" in *West Side Story*. I was successful in stopping myself from becoming enraged by this aspect of my situation, this idea that I needed to deal with a probation officer. This was part of the whole thing and, as Levine had told me in advance, you start going down this road and you've got to go all the way. Okay.

So I went off to see my probation officer, whose office is in the Courthouse. That at least was a blessing; if I ran into anyone, if I was seen by some journalist, they had no way of knowing I was not seeing some judge or involved in some other prestigious activity. There was no special side door of the Courthouse that said, "Criminals Enter Here."

The U.S. Probation Service offices are on the second floor of the Courthouse, and the offices themselves are moderately decrepit, filled with low-grade federal government furniture. Sitting in the waiting room I read very old magazines and one highly salacious pamphlet on AIDS prevention.

I had met my probation officer briefly on October 7, but we hadn't talked much. This was my real initiation into the criminal justice system. Gregory A. Hunt was about forty-five or fifty, gray-haired, with a beard and mustache. His office was medium-size and crowded, it seemed to me, with filing cabinets and furniture. I sat across the desk from him, and we got started.

I knew this man was important to me, for he would write up my case in a report to the judge that would influence the sentence I got. He would in fact recommend a sentence and I understood that in about 75 percent of these cases, judges would follow the recommendation of the probation officer. It was bizarre. We had shaken hands once, this man and I, he knew almost nothing about me, and he was now one of the most important people in my life.

So it was a relief and a tonic to find that he was a man of decency and competence. He began asking for basic data about me, like data of birth, height, weight. As to the last, I answered, "About ten pounds less than it was a month ago." Yeah, he said, I don't see people at their best in this job; people are pretty down. My friends ask me why I do it. Well, I said, why do you do it? Because, he answered, it's a place where I can do something about a really bad actor when I meet one, and where if I find a decent guy, I can cut him a deal. Good answer, I thought; if my answers are as good as his, I'll be all right.

So what happened? he asked after a while. How did all this happen?

Good question.

I knew I could not "let go," and say, well, this happened because Reagan was too cowardly and so he appointed a special prosecutor, and this happened because the goddamn Democrats on the Hill decided to try to win in criminal courts what they cannot win at the polls, and this happened because Craig Gillen wants to run for governor some day. Nope. Not wise.

So I said something equally true and less volatile. This happened because we were at war, we and the Democrats in Congress, or so we thought and they thought. There were sometimes hearings where they asked fair, decent, intelligent questions whose purpose was to find out the truth. Hearings on Haiti, Jamaica, earthquake aid, or religious freedom in Cuba. But on Central America, hearings were a form of combat. Questions were weapons, and answers were shields. So when I was asked for information that might help them, might give them yet more ammunition, I tried to deny it to them. I tried to figure out how I could give them the least information possible.

Or rather, legally possible. I never thought I was violating the law. Never. It never occurred to me. If it had, I would not have given those answers; we tried desperately hard and spent huge amounts of time, trying to stay within the law. No one ever suggested to me it might be possible that my testimony was unlawful. Maybe if the answers to questions had been written I'd have realized I should not give them; maybe if I had had time to think I would have thought better of it. But the Q and A was oral, and there was no time to reflect, only to parry, only to jump and stab and duck. I said that no foreign government, "was helping" the Contras, because the money from Brunei had not arrived; if and when it arrived I knew I'd have to stop saying that, but for the moment that formulation seemed safe, if tricky.

As to North, I never knew of any illegal activity on his part, or for that matter anyone else's, never knew about Iran, never knew about the diversion. I thought what the congressmen were really getting at in their questions was illegal activity, especially direction or operation of that private network, and I was happy to deny that. Clearly the denial was much too broad, because it denied not only that North ran the private network, but even that he'd had any contacts with it. Again, I think I'd have seen that if the testimony had been prepared in advance, I'd have struck that language. But I said what I said, and it's too late now.

Hunt was a decent and intelligent man, and he knew the kind of horror this conviction represented to me and to my family. His questions about State, CIA, and DOD; about North, Fiers, Shultz, and Reagan; about Nicaragua, Congress, and the Administration showed he was trying to grasp the facts as quickly as he could. Unlike Gillen, he had no ax to grind. I had pleaded guilty, so that was over. The issue now was, who was I? Other than this crime, what had I been doing for the last ten years? How did it all fit together?

A home visit is part of this, he explained. I don't know what my face showed, but the idea at first made me gag. Jesus Christ! A home visit! To see if there's crack cocaine around in the bathroom? To see if we have guns in the kitchen drawers? But that feeling passed, largely because Hunt said, look, it may not seem useful in this kind of case, but it is; you and I can talk some more, and I can talk to your wife.

THURSDAY, OCTOBER 17

Rachel's Jeremiad

Hunt came by the following week, and we sat around the dining room table and talked. We had asked him to come between nine and three, so as not to be there when the kids were home, and he had readily agreed. Best-laid plans department: Jacob wasn't feeling well that day, so he was at home. But it wasn't a problem. He stayed upstairs happily watching TV and came down only to shake hands.

Hunt began by saying to us, and especially to Rachel, I am not your enemy. I am here to talk, to find out more about your husband and your family, about what happened and how it is affecting you.

It was strange: he was the first government official we had come across in this entire process who was not posturing. He was asking questions because he actually wanted to know the answers. I tried to remember the last time that had happened, and I could not think back far enough.

This was a great opportunity for Rachel to participate, to act, to have an effect on the outcome of these judicial processes. She talked at length, and in fact the home visit turned out to be mostly a conversation between her and Hunt. So, far from being stupid, far from being another product of this incomprehensible mess and the tangles of a hopeless legal system, it was in fact a useful couple of hours—for Hunt, I think, and certainly for Rachel. She talked about me, about the children, about the years at State—about everything, and in ways I could not, and with insights I did not have.

It had an impact; you would have had to be made of stone, you would have had to be insensate for it not to. It was curious. A part of this legal process that had seemed most ludicrous, most demeaning, even humiliating, and certainly useless, was turning out to be a rare corner of humanity and common sense. Why? How could this be, I wondered. And then it became clear: this part has nothing to do with politics. So it can be done straightforwardly and honestly.

But Rachel's true feelings were too strong to express in conversation, with Hunt or anyone else, so she sat down and wrote them out and sent them off to her closest friend. The letter came out of the typewriter smoking. It began this way:

Dearest J—

I am sitting here going mad, crawling out of my skin, feeling this worm of rage turning, turning inside me, and I don't know what to do with it. I don't think you really understand what this is about, so I will make an effort to explain it.

I'll start from the end: In just a few days we will go before the Chief Judge of the United States District Court for the District of Columbia, to hear what punishment he will mete out to Elliott for his crime. Do you recall having forms in front of you which ask you: Have you ever been convicted of a crime? If so, what crime? You've seen those questions and never paused over them. But from November 15 onward, forever, when he gets to those questions, Elliott will have to answer: yes, I have been convicted of a crime. A misdemeanor crime. 2 U.S.C. 192. Contempt of Congress. It's a big joke, isn't it? Contempt of Congress! Who doesn't feel it? Who hasn't expressed it openly a thousand times? Can it really be a crime to scorn and condemn those back-slapping, ass-pinching (yes, Anita), name-calling, soul-selling

UNDUE PROCESS

worms in human form? Can it really be a crime to withhold information from the likes of them? But maybe you don't get it, because you
don't live here, because you've never lived in this city.

Think of a sinkhole; peer in: here are the loathsome eels and their
loathsome toadies overrunning the Congress; here are the rats gnaw-
ing at each other in the maze of Presidential appointments; here are
the horseflies and mosquitoes who are pleased to call themselves
attorneys, the lawyers and lawyerettes, hum-hum-humming, hover-
ing, inhaling blood and money; here are the carrion-eaters of the
press corps, who daily take their meals at the flesh of the fallen
mighty. And there are the fools, like my husband, who dream of
entering here without abandoning all hope.

I entered here, this concrete-covered swamp, almost twelve years
ago, left New York and all behind me, brimming with hope. I was
married to this golden man, my prize. And here I am, clenching,
grinding, my teeth, wondering how to save him from, how to hurt,
how to savage, how to kill, the people who have called him a
criminal.

It's a joke among Elliott's lawyers, how I feel. They never neglect
to remind me to behave decorously: down girl, down! But really it's
no joke to me that I live in a place where a certain kind of lie, the lie
of the Act, is the accepted, the expected, the demanded behavior.
Have I hurt you, snubbed you, abandoned you, uttered imprecations
against you, fouled your name? No hard feelings, it's only politics.
What is a friend here? There are some real friends here, true friends;
but, see, here is a place where friendship will find itself forced to
express itself in letters to a judge, asking him to be lenient in his
sentence. For the others, they can come and go with the wind.
You're up? I kiss your face en route to your ass. You're down? I kiss
you off.

Even for Elliott's lawyers, and he has a boy-scout troop of them, the
lie of the Act can mean a lot. Oh, our lawyers; oh the hours upon
hours of logged time they've given us. I recognize that my anger at
them is unfair. They are not our enemies, I know that. It's only that

it will never be in their nature, it can't be in their nature, to understand what I believe, to see the world with my eyes, to see all this as a battle between right and wrong, maybe even Good and Evil, to see that wrong has won this skirmish, that there are hard feelings, and that they don't go away.

I've never laid eyes on Walsh in the flesh, but I have seen the face of his toady, Craig Gillen, and I tell you he is thrillingly alive to me as an object of my poison hatred. On the day of Elliott's arraignment, October 7, he awaits us in the holding room at the U.S. Courthouse, together with three of his minions: "I am the assistant to the assistant to the assistant to the man who is the deputy to the prosecutor in this case." Where are you, Gilbert and Sullivan, when I need you?

In the morning, before we leave the house, the press buzzards are circling outside our door, cameras in tow. How do they know? Who tells them to perch themselves around our house on this particular day waiting for their piece of meat? One of them ventures to ring the bell, to get his own private little nip of Elliott before the others, caw, caw, descend, but gets a hot blast from me instead for his pains. Ah, but no hard feelings, that's business, it's only politics.

They swarm outside the courthouse, too; are there hard feelings when I elbow the gut of one who shoves his camera in my face? Can you know how desperately I pray that there are? How very much I want to hurt this vulture, physically hurt him?

So Gillen awaits us, salivating, in this squalid holding room, and he greets Elliott, his prize, the man for whose sake he has willingly left behind his home, given up his family, for months on end; his snare, his catch, his victim, his scalp, the man he and others just like him have dogged for their employer, their career-making employer, for five years. He is proud of this success. It shows up in the brief icy smile he gives as we arrive. But he doesn't greet me. He won't look into my eyes. I stare and stare and stare at him, but he doesn't look at me. I spend the eternal half hour it takes for Elliott to plead guilty in that courtroom, staring at Craig Gillen. My eyes burn with the effort, and I can't unglue them from him, but he won't look at me.

U N D U E   P R O C E S S

I shout at him inside my head, "You son of a bitch, fuck you fuck you fuck you, you son of a bitch!" at such tremendous, thundering, pitch, I wonder if I am actually saying it out loud, if he can hear it. He can't hear it, but he hears it anyway. He doesn't look at me.

And the lie of the Act is there, too. This Craig Gillen, whose career as a prosecutor has been secured by his snatching of my husband, whose political ambition will be furthered by it, this specimen of tight ass and compressed lips, this pretty-boy, blond, Georgia WASP, this loathsome little toady of Lawrence Walsh's, and his minions, too, they receive us there in that courthouse, our gracious hosts, shaking hands all around. Not mine—I would sooner touch putrescent liver. But elsewhere hands are shaken, even Elliott's, I fear, though I don't look. The shaking of hands: yes, this is civilized. No hard feelings, it's only politics. This is where I live.

In the maddening, mad, swelling voice in my head there is rebellion, a demand for action, some kind of action. How am I to answer it? This is all about withholding information from the abominable, bloated, check-kiting, drunken, eelish, foul, greedy, hypocritical, ignorant, jelly-legged, keel-hauling, lying, mindless, nictitating, obtuse, pusillanimous, quaking, ruthless, simpering, treacherous, useless, vile, whoring, xenophobic, yellow-bellied, zeros who populate the Congress. What? Only withhold information from them? Arrest them! Manacle them! Hang them! Electrocute them!

I can't get satisfaction. There isn't any of the kind of revenge I want to be had. I don't want to wait for thirty years, or thirty days, a la Siciliana, or even three days, to eat that plate cold. I want it hot, searing, roiling, boiling, third-degree-burn hot, and I want it now.

Walsh Shoots High

They want to see you again, Pierson had told me. Who "they" was could not have been clearer: Gillen & Company. Why? For a discussion; not an interview with notes, no FBI, just a talk about their favorite subjects. Elliott has told you everything he did and why he did it ten times, Pierson had replied; but Gillen had said, no, we want to talk about other people this time. We want to go over what he knows about the involvement of others. But he has already been over that ten times, too, Pierson had protested, and Gillen had replied that they would see if anything more came back to me.

I fumed, all the more because it was hopeless to think of resisting. I called Peter Morgan to ask if I could somehow not do this, but he said no. Look, he said, you have two weeks to sentencing. Don't play games. The truth is that you don't have any information about anyone else that might harm them. Just tell the truth, and don't go speculating and reaching and theorizing. You're lucky, he said: you can tell the truth and not get anyone in trouble. Be happy with that.

I was not happy, although what Morgan said was clearly right. I was not happy because I hated facing Gillen with that mask of civility,

179

hated facing him and spending hours with him without being able to say, I'll answer your questions because I have to, but it makes me sick to sit in the same room with you. So I put on my act again, and I was just the nicest, friendliest, most cooperative fellow you ever did meet. What did they want? Simple. They only wanted one thing: George Bush.

For two hours they asked me about Don Gregg, who had for the eight Reagan years been Bush's National Security Adviser. I had already told them I remembered nothing about Gregg that would advance their prosecution. Gregg had never been in my office. I had never been in Gregg's office. We had spoken on the phone perhaps once a year, perhaps twice. But boy oh boy did they want Don Gregg, and they tried to "help" my memory a little. They unearthed every single point where Gregg's path and mine had crossed in the 1980s: every meeting we both had attended, every list we both appeared on, every reference to both of our names in someone's memo. Didn't that help me remember? Didn't that jog something in my mind? Nope. It was a calm, relaxed afternoon, just a bunch of guys sitting around trying to see if they could start something up that would end in impeaching the President.

WEDNESDAY, OCTOBER 30

Craig Writes a Letter

My answers on Don Gregg had seemed to sadden them, but not to surprise them, and I anticipated no hostile reaction on their part. And maybe the letter they sent to Hunt, the probation officer, on October 30 was not hostile; maybe it was their idea of fairness, accuracy, and truth.

It is customary for a probation officer to ask the prosecutors for a statement of facts, for a fleshed-out version of the case that might tell more than the Statement of Facts presented at the arraignment. And it is customary for the prosecutors to reply with a letter or memo that tells more of the story. Fairly. Accurately.

But maybe those are just a few more of the usual rules that don't seem to bind Special Prosecutors. Gillen's letter to Hunt infuriated me; it even surprised me. I had actually persuaded myself that Walsh and his boys had gotten their pound of flesh, gotten their scalp, and would now lay off me. Instead they presented a version of facts, particularly regarding Count Two, the Brunci count, that was just plain unfair.

"In December 1985," they wrote to Hunt, "Congress authorized the Department of State to solicit third countries to obtain humanitarian

181

assistance for the Contras.'' Fair enough, I thought; they are acknowledging that the solicitation itself was clearly legal. Then they went on, ''In the Summer of 1986, Mr. Abrams discussed with Secretary of State George P. Shultz the possibility of soliciting the Sultan of Brunei for contra support.''

Hold it! My kids get magazines with games that say, ''What's missing in this picture?'' I played that game here. How come there's no mention that this process did not begin with *me,* but with a May 1986 NSC meeting at which the President and his Cabinet officers discussed whether to turn to third countries? How come there's no mention that the President decided, not me? Are they trying to make this seem like some Lone Ranger effort of mine?

The next paragraph of Gillen's letter answered that question: ''Elliott Abrams played an active role in soliciting a contribution from the Sultan of Brunei. In August 1986 Mr Abrams went to London under an assumed name to meet with a representative of the Sultan. During a meeting in a park in London, Mr. Abrams requested a substantial contribution for the Contras and gave the Sultan's representative the number of a Swiss bank account (obtained from North) into which the contribution could be deposited. In mid-September 1986, Mr. Abrams learned that the Sultan had agreed to make the contribution. Shortly before the end of September 1986, Mr. Abrams was informed that the Sultan had sent the money to North's account.'' End of story.

This was unbelievable. It had major factual errors, and all of them were designed to push the probation officer into the gravest possible conclusion about my conduct. And to the extent that what they said was correct, it was incomplete. Which meant, I said to myself, that Walsh and Gillen were . . . . . . *withholding information*!

First of all, this cloak-and-dagger garbage designed, again, to make me seem as much as possible like Ollie North or their idea of a CIA agent: ''Abrams went to London under an assumed name.'' Cute, dramatic, and false. And they knew it. They had all the documents: my State Department travel orders, made out for Elliott Abrams. My diplomatic passport, stamped with the Heathrow Airport arrival and departure in London. My Pan Am Ticket, in my name. My London Hilton hotel bill, in my name.

This business was not new. at the Iran/Contra hearings, Senator Cohen had raised this incognito travel, and I had told him it was not true, and that he and the Committee staff had the documents to prove it. Okay, he had said. Then he had written a book about the Iran/Contra affair, and in it he had said, Abrams traveled to London under an assumed name. So much for fairness and accuracy. And now, here we go again.

Then the dates, wrong in a way that put me in the worst possible false light. The Government of Brunei, Gillen & Company knew, because they had all the cables, had made a promise to the United States in August. But the money did not arrive. Days went by, weeks went by, and the money did not arrive. When I testified on October 10, we expected the money, we thought it would come sooner or later, but it had not arrived. That is precisely why I thought I could say no foreign government was at that time helping the Contras. Yes, one had secretly promised to help, but at the time I testified I thought not one cent of foreign government money was sustaining the Contras.

But you wouldn't get any of that from what Gillen had written. He didn't say, the President decided this, and soliciting third countries was certainly not Abrams's idea. He didn't say, Shultz authorized every action taken. He didn't say, every communication was made via State Department cable to the U.S. Embassy in Brunei. He didn't say, not a nickel from Brunei had arrived when Abrams testified.

What was going on here? I wondered. A criminal conviction wasn't enough for them; now they were twisting the evidence and withholding information from the probation officer to make it all seem worse. Why? No one would see their letter, it wouldn't be made public, its only possible effect would be on sentencing.

You are a naïve person, I thought to myself. Boy, are you a chump. Once upon a time you thought that they'd play fair with you, and even their decision to force you into a criminal court didn't persuade you otherwise. You are actually surprised they want you to rot in hell. You are astonished they want the probation officer and the judge to think you're a bum and throw the book at you.

Yes, I was astonished. And I thought of what Joseph N. Welch had said to Joe McCarthy at the Army–McCarthy hearings: "Have you no sense of decency, sir? At long last, have you left no sense of decency?"

Back to the Grand Jury

The Grand Jury, from 10 A.M. to 4 P.M.

As a lawyer, I know the history. The grand jury is a protection for citizens, a constitutional barrier to prosecutors, a safeguard against tyranny. The Fifth Amendment says: "No person shall be held to answer for a capital, or otherwise infamous crime, unless on a presentment or indictment of a Grand Jury." But God save us and protect us, because the grand jury sure won't. Here were twenty-four men and women (women, mostly), the majority of whom could not have been less interested in the questions or the answers. Several were asleep most of the time, several more were asleep part of the time, several others were visibly not paying attention, and virtually all were deeply engaged only when the discussion turned on getting their break or going to lunch.

I don't blame them and I don't criticize them, because they got the point: they are a decoration. They have no real role. One hears about runaway grand juries, but mostly in the movies. In fact the grand jurors do not speak, do not question the witness, do not do anything. The prosecutor asked me questions, and I answered them, he looking at me, and me looking at him. It was a bit rude, I suppose, to those poor twenty-four people, but I figured they wouldn't blame me for it.

What did we spend those hours on? Repetition. I had answered most of the questions in the fall of 1986, in 1987, in 1988, and more recently in the fall of 1991. The answers hadn't changed. The prosecutors' purpose was to get me to incriminate other people, and they seemed unsurprised but still a bit disappointed that I couldn't do so; they whispered to each other and shrugged quite a lot. The best parts were the questions like, "You spoke to Oliver North on the telephone on October 8, 1986. What did you say to him?" That one was my personal favorite, but there were many ties for second and third.

Gillen had started by saying, You are here pursuant to your plea agreement and your agreement in it to cooperate, aren't you? No, I had said; I have always cooperated with every investigation, and this is my fourth grand jury appearance. Well, but, he had said, this is pursuant to a plea agreement, isn't it? No, I had repeated; I'd be here without it; I always cooperate with any legitimate investigation. At which he had given up and said, Well, anyway, you're here. A small victory for my side.

Still, it was horrible. I did not want to be there at all, but my lawyers correctly said, Don't fool around before your sentencing. So I showed up, without asking for any immunity, without taking the Fifth or anything else, and—of course—without my lawyer. Pierson was in the Courthouse, upstairs, where I could reach him if need be—if something big enough arose and I said, Stop! Halt! I need my lawyer. In reality that provided me, as it does all witnesses, comfort without assistance. Not only does the grand jury not protect you, it actually hurts you, for it is one of the few dangerous places left where you can't have a lawyer.

Gillen had, before I had gone into the grand jury room, offered Pierson a kind of apology for his letter to the probation officer, saying he did not mean to suggest, had not meant to imply, blah blah blah. I guess he felt he had gone too far.

The feeling didn't last, however.

THURSDAY, NOVEMBER 7

Leaks

I awoke the following day and found the following item in the *Washington Times*: "Special prosecutors questioned former Assistant Secretary of State Elliott Abrams yesterday trying to implicate in the scandal a former aide to President Bush, sources said. Prosecutors also subpoenaed former White House aide Oliver North as part of the effort to show Iran–Contra involvement by Donald Gregg, now U.S. Ambassador to South Korea. . . . Two sources described the North subpoena and questioning of Mr. Abrams before a federal grand jury as a last-ditch effort to show that Mr. Gregg has been covering up his knowledge of the affair . . ."

Were they leaking again?

It got worse. I complained to Pierson, who told me a wire service reporter had called him the previous night, just hours after my testimony, to tell him what I had been asked about. He had had it right. Goddamn, I thought; they are really hitting the phones.

What could we do? Until Friday the 15th, not much. Ask them, accuse them, and they'd just deny everything. And we had no "proof," none. Now if you could investigate, if you could put good old Craig in front of a grand jury, if you could get an Independent Counsel appointed! Sauce for the goose, I thought to myself, but they knew, as I knew, that they were safe. The only person, so far as I could remember, who had ever been punished for leaking was Charles Colson of the Nixon Administration, and that only proved the point.

Leaking is never viewed as morally good or bad, intrinsically; it all depends on whether the leaker or the leakee is good or bad, and that decision is made, a priori, by the press and sometimes by the Congress. No one was going to punish Lawrence Walsh's staff for leaking.

Anyway, no time to sit around and sulk, we had work to do. We had to finish off our memo to the judge about sentencing.

This document turned out to be a work of law, politics, and art, in equal parts. It told the story of my life, of my crimes, of my public career; it explained the context for my testimony in October 1986 and tried to put it in the best light possible; it reviewed sentences in related cases and asked for leniency.

I wrote the first draft, for so much of the information was personal, and I liked doing it. I was at least doing *something* to help myself. Then Pierson and Morgan refined and rewrote it, and added the section about sentencing, and Rachel and I became the editors. Here the task was very depressing, for I was reading and rereading the sections about how much damage this whole affair had done to my life, my career, my future. I understood the game: you stress this, of course, you dwell on it, because you are asking the judge to be lenient. "He has suffered enough" is the main theme. Still, you cannot lie or stretch the truth, and there it was: a cold assessment of what these five years had meant, and what the criminal conviction had already added to them. As I assayed my own future, I could not shake the weight of that section. Maybe it was not just "true," but absolutely true.

We reviewed all the relevant sentences. Under Section 192, no one had ever gone to jail; some sentences in other 192 cases had ranged as low as probation for a few months and a $100 fine, to probation for a year and a $2,000 fine. Bud McFarlane was the closest case, because he had pleaded to four Section 192 counts and had received a $20,000 fine and two hundred hours of community service, plus two years' probation. If you divided by two for my two counts, I might get half.

In other Iran/Contra cases, Secord had pleaded to one felony count and gotten only probation, not even a fine; Hakim had received two years' probation and a $5,000 fine. North had been convicted of three felony counts and been sentenced to two years' probation, 1,200 hours of community service, and a $150,000 fine. Poindexter had been found guilty of five felony counts and been sentenced to jail for six months.

However, and it was a big however, North was now off scot-free. He had demanded immunity before testifying before Congress, and had gotten it, and now that immunity had made it possible for his conviction to be thrown out. It seemed likely Poindexter would reach the same result.

So the likeliest result for me seemed to be $10,000 in fines and one hundred hours of community service. Maybe a bit more. Who could tell what the judge would think? There were letters to him recounting my work in the Human Rights Bureau and my career in government, pointing out that I had not gone off to Wall Street to spend the 1980s making millions. My wife wrote to him, as the lawyers suggested she do, and her letter was so brilliant, so moving, so filled with love that I felt it was almost worth the whole prosecution just to have such a letter written about me. Would he conclude I had in fact been penalized enough, especially given that North and Poindexter were going to walk away from it all? Would he say, No, you're a lawyer, and a lesson must be taught here, and throw the book at me?

And what did that mean? Jail? The probation officer had told me Judge Robinson didn't believe jail helped anyone, that he sentenced people to jail only when they really had to be taken off the streets for the safety of the community. I could not bring myself to take the idea of jail seriously. True, this whole thing was Kafkaesque; given what had transpired up to now, why should another bizarre chapter be impossible? But I could not think about it, for one simple reason: the kids. Both being separated from them and the effect of it all on them were simply too much. It was sensory overload; my brain shut down. And that was sensible, too, given the percentages; no one thought jail was any kind of a possibility.

I could not stop myself from pursuing, mentally, the other extreme: escape. Maybe the judge would give me probation only. Or a really light sentence, like a few thousand in fines and no community service. I could not change my feeling about community service, that it was penal servitude itself, slave labor. I would do it if I had to, but with resentment. I hoped for, dreamed of, a sentence of probation.

Once in a while I would stop and say, Jesus Christ, *hoping* for probation! Probation! Report in to your probation officer, now; mark it on your calendar so you don't forget. Do I have to ask permission to leave Washington? To go abroad? And this would go on for two years? It would be almost 1994 before I was free of this? Unbelievable. For testimony given in October 1986, I would be reporting to a probation officer in November 1993.

Stop. Stop now, I told myself. What is the purpose of this little mental game? Go do something useful, like drafting the statement you have to make in court on the day of the sentencing. Which is what I did.

WEDNESDAY, NOVEMBER 13

The Courthouse Steps, in Draft

S ay this for Craig Gillen: he never disappoints.

The probation officer's report to the judge was good for me. It said positive things about my contributions as a government official, and its review of the facts of the case was fair. It accepted neither my version nor the prosecution's as gospel, and while I had expected this, apparently old Craig had not. He flipped out, and wrote a three-page, single-spaced letter to Gregory Hunt instructing him in the errors of his ways.

I knew Gillen's line on the prosecution would be "we just had to set the record straight," but he went far beyond that. His letter, first of all, stated that I had "last week acknowledged for the first time" before the grand jury some new facts about what North had told the RIG, with a clear implication that I had previously been lying and had only now come clean. That was simply false: what I had told the grand jury was just what I'd been saying for five years, namely that North had told people things about the private operation but had never revealed that he ran it. Gillen's letter said North and Fiers claimed they remembered North telling the RIG all sorts of facts about the private network, but conve-

191

niently left out that a dozen other RIG members had no such memory. His letter certainly raised questions about my veracity, and about the degree to which I was truly accepting responsibility for my acts.

And this letter was delivered two days before sentencing. Was it, could it possibly be, an attempt to influence the sentence, to guard against leniency? If Gillen were writing only to set the record straight, why could he not wait until after the sentencing to do so? The Special Prosecutor's office seemed to attract people who never let fairness or moderation interfere when they had a chance to do some real damage to anyone.

I began to draft the statements I would use on the courthouse steps.

The first draft, perhaps reflecting my anger at Gillen, was the toughest attack on the OIC.

First Draft: Statement for Courthouse Steps

I have a brief statement, and then I'll take a few questions.

I want to express my gratitude to Gregory Hunt of the US Probation Service, and to Chief Judge Robinson of the US District Court, for their very fair treatment of me throughout the last few weeks. Given the situation I was in when they met me, I believe they sought to treat me justly.

But I do not believe I have been treated justly by the Special Prosecutor, Lawrence Walsh, or by his staff.

First, I have been the subject of literally dozens of leaks by that office over the last several years, the most recent of which was only last week. I can hardly think of a situation that calls more powerfully for a Special Prosecutor, than that kind of abuse by the Office of the Special Prosecutor itself. It is unfair to individuals being investigated, and it is a terrible abuse of the power vested in that office. I hope that before Congress votes these people another dime, someone will ask about this pattern of leaking.

Second, I do not believe it was accidental that, after three years in which they did not contact me even once, that Office decided to move against me only when the North case was thrown out. I believe their motivation was personal and political vindication, not justice. They read the criticisms after they lost the North case, saying "5 years and 50 million dollars, and nothing to show for it," and de cided they needed a scalp.

Finally, I would remind you that this country survived and prospered for two hundred and ten years without the criminalization of political and policy disputes. The notion that Executive Branch officials' unsworn testimony on policy issues should be thrown into the criminal justice system is an innovation brought to us by Lawrence Walsh. For two hundred and ten years before my testimony, witnesses have had to do what I did: judge which of the facts in your head on a given day to divulge to the Congress. To testify is to choose what to say and what not to say, and until Mr. Walsh came along no one had ever argued that that choice is always a criminal, rather than a political, matter.

I think you all know that during the five years since my testimony, witnesses have continued to make those choices, to divulge some facts and not divulge others. We see it on television and read about it in the newspapers every day, and those witnesses are—rightly— criticized and defended for their testimony—but not told that it will become the subject of a criminal investigation.

So the standards have not changed, and the behavior of witnesses has not changed, and it never will. It should not. Executive Branch witnesses will defend the policies of their Administration, and opposing Congressmen will attack them. This case does not teach the lesson that you must reveal everything you know to Congress, because your brain is not a filing cabinet you can hand over. A witness inevitably must select what to say.

And this case does not establish precise standards as to what a witness must divulge. If you think of all the testimony, some of it now famous testimony, in the last few months, it is clear that there is not and cannot be a clear standard as to precisely what a witness must say. And that's precisely the problem: if you can't figure out in advance what testimony will be prosecuted and what will not, if there are no standards and no precedents, if you can't determine which facts must be divulged and which may be protected, you aren't really functioning in a system of law at all. You are functioning in a system where political vengeance is the controlling principle.

The lesson here is simple. The lesson is that a Special Prosecutor who decides he needs victims will create victims. The lesson is that when political disagreements are thrown into the criminal justice system, both the character of our political system, and the integrity of our system of justice, are damaged. And this is especially true when the Special Prosecutor acts to vindicate his own budget and his own longevity.

The lesson is simple, and the solutions are simple. Let the Justice Department and the US Attorneys do their jobs. Fight out political fights in the Congress, not in the courts. Separate policy disputes from criminal conduct. And do not, ever again, allow a small group of people determined to advance their careers, and to justify their waste of time and of public money, to pervert the criminal laws to serve their personal and political ends.

I debated whether this was the right move. It would sound bitter, vindictive. Was that the image I wanted? It was probably too personal, too, in the attacks. I needed something tonier, something more political science-ish, something that would make arguments other people might be interested in. Besides, my lawyers would never let me get away with the first draft. Too provocative, they would say. So I tried again.

Second Draft: Statement for Courthouse Steps

I have a brief statement. At an appropriate time I will have more to say about all this, probably in writing.

I want to express my gratitude to Gregory Hunt of the US Probation Service, and to Chief Judge Robinson of the US District Court, for their very fair treatment of me throughout the last few weeks. Given the situation I was in when they met me, I believe they sought to treat me justly.

UNDUE PROCESS

As you would expect, I have a less enthusiastic view of my treatment by the Special Prosecutor, Lawrence Walsh, and his staff.

For two hundred and fifteen years, witnesses have necessarily been judging what facts to divulge to the Congress. There are no precise standards, which is fine in political discourse but grave if criminal sanctions are to be applied. If a witness cannot be certain in advance what testimony will be prosecuted and what will not, if there are no standards and no precedents, if it is extremely difficult to determine which facts must be divulged and which may be protected, we aren't really functioning in a system of *law* at all. And that is why the criminal laws have never been applied to such Executive Branch testimony. The criminalization of political and policy disputes—the notion that Executive Branch officials' unsworn testimony on policy issues should be thrown into the criminal justice system—is an innovation, a new theory introduced by the present Special Prosecutor. I think it is a very bad one.

The lack of standards means there is an enormous area of prosecutorial discretion, and it is made even larger, and less predictable, when it is vested in a Special Prosecutor's office that is not in fact part of the usual system of restraints of the Department of Justice and the US Attorneys' offices. The pattern that emerges is that, out of all the people involved in a particular policy dispute, and out of all those who testify before Congress over a period of years, a small group is targeted for prosecution. Neither the Special Prosecutor, nor anyone else, can really say why all of these individuals, but only these individuals, were selected, and no-one can accurately describe the prosecutorial standards future witnesses will face.

That is not a system of law, as we usually use the term, and I believe we weaken both our political system and our criminal justice system by proceeding this way.

Now, that was better. Less personal, more general. Less bitter. It made the argument. But Len Garment called to say, don't use it. You still don't make it clear enough, he said, that these are public policy issues, issues that transcend the fate of Elliott Abrams. Talk more about the effect of these prosecutions on government, on how government operates. You run the risk of sounding tricky, sounding as if you were penitent in the courtroom and then raced outside to reverse your position. This seemed good advice, and my third draft was even better.

Third Draft: Statement for Courthouse Steps

I have a brief statement.

I want to express my gratitude to Gregory Hunt of the US Probation Service, and to Chief Judge Robinson of the US District Court, for their very fair treatment of me throughout the last few weeks. Given the situation I was in when they met me, I believe they sought to treat me justly. I would also like to express my appreciation to the many friends, colleagues, and other Americans who have come forward in the past weeks to offer me their support.

This prosecution, and all of the others brought by the Office of Independent Counsel, raise serious and important questions about the process of government. They are a major departure from past practice in our country, because they criminalize political differences. They stand for the proposition that the unsworn testimony of Executive Branch officials on policy issues should be the subject of criminal action. Until this Special Prosecutor came along, no such case was ever brought in the history of the United States. Such a deviation from the American political tradition is bound to affect the way the government operates, and that is a complex subject I plan to address in the future.

Because this kind of prosecution is something new in America, there are few standards that govern the Office of Independent Counsel in bringing these cases. No-one, I believe, can really explain how the present Independent Counsel exercises his immensely broad prosecutorial discretion. No-one can accurately describe the prosecutorial standards future Executive Branch witnesses will face—particularly if they are going to face new Independent Counsels. When will withholding information from Congress, which is what I did, be treated as a crime? How will it be decided which witnesses to prosecute, and which to pass by? Unless these questions are answered the same way each time they are raised, we are not operating in a system of law at all. All this should make the Independent Counsel careful and discreet in his prosecutorial conduct, a test I believe the current incumbent has failed. This in itself is a significant question deserving careful attention, and again, I will address it in the future.

And now, with this behind me, I'm happy to get back to work.

Now this was what I really wanted to say. There was more, of course, but that could be in the Q & A. For example, I wanted to ask: if you were appointed today as an Assistant Secretary, and you asked someone to study my case, and the Gates and Thomas hearings, and advise you what the current standards are for withholding information, what would the answer be? It would be, search me! There are no standards. In which case, how can you fairly prosecute someone?

But the real question was, should I say anything at all on the steps. My father-in-law argued against it, saying that I had no control over what the TV or press would carry and might be very unhappy with the excerpts they chose. Wheras, he said, in an op ed piece or magazine article I could present a reasoned argument in my own words. Fair points. My cousin Floyd Abrams argued that I was at my least credible on these issues standing on the steps immediately after sentencing. Moreover, he said, if you say all this the story will be "Abrams Attacks Walsh," and that doesn't help you. If you say almost nothing, they'll have to cover the sentencing hearing, where the only substantive speaker will be your lawyer.

Good advice. Pierson and Morgan agreed with it, and when I reached Levine he did too. I was disappointed; the first draft didn't even convey half the anger I felt, stepped up again now by Gillen's letter to Hunt. What a system! They attack and attack, they kick and punch and maul and bite, and you have to worry about appearing sober and restrained in the press. Okay, I will, I figured. I'll just say, This case raises a lot of serious and important issues about our government, and I will be addressing them in the coming days and weeks. In other words, I'm not talking today, but stay tuned.

Pierson then called; he had been to see Gillen. Gillen had claimed, of course, he just had to set the record straight. They had some notes indicating North had told the RIG things about his activities, and they had to say that. Just had to. But, Pierson had said, what was this business about "Abrams last week acknowledged for the first time"? Gillen had seemed somewhat apologetic. Last week in the grand jury, Elliott was more specific than he had ever been before, Gillen had said. Gillen had seemed to agree that maybe his characterization, his words, had gone overboard, but it didn't seem to him a big, serious deal. Look, Pierson had said, you set this in motion, I didn't. Now we have to deal with it. We think this is a bum rap, this "last week for the first time" bit, and we don't want any implication that Elliott had been hiding things and was coming clean now. Second, we don't want any implication that Elliott is refusing responsibility for his acts. That just isn't so.

Oh no, Gillen had said, we're not implying that. That's not a problem. So Gillen had got Gregory Hunt on the line, and with Pierson sitting there had told him they weren't really urging this point that I had said something for the first time. And then he had told Hunt they were not at all implying I had not fully accepted responsibility for my acts; on the contrary, their position was that I had.

They have done this twice now, I thought to myself. The day of my grand jury appearance, November 6, Gillen had more or less apologized to Pierson for some of the "facts" he had communicated to Hunt about my actions back in 1986. You might think that would have made him behave better, but you'd have been wrong. Their theory seems to be, shoot first and apologize later. This is great behavior for a prosecutor, I thought: damage people in any way you can, and if their lawyer is adamant enough, appear slightly sheepish. After the damage is done.

Was there damage? It wasn't clear. Hunt said he had to tell the judge about this disagreement; maybe we should delay sentencing. No! Pierson and Gillen had both said. Instead Hunt was going to write a short letter to the judge telling him—neutrally—about this dispute. He'd say, the OIC says there are notes of a RIG suggesting North told a lot about his activities, but not suggesting that Abrams knew of any illegal activities. What a stupid mess. And a dangerous one, if the judge misread it.

With this in mind, Pierson had asked Gillen what he planned to say in court the next day. Very little, Gillen had answered. He'd just say that I had cooperated fully, testified whenever asked, and conducted myself in a highly professional manner. And, I thought, he might even say that, and only that, if he actually feels he overstepped in his letter to Hunt.

We'd soon find out.

As the day progressed, I was increasingly nervous. There were no hard reasons to be: all the signs pointed to a decent outcome. Hunt's report, Gillen's likely statement in Court, our own submission to the judge, the letters to the judge—all suggested a decent outcome, in the terms I was by then defining as decent. Robinson had sentenced not only McFarlane but also Secord, and despite the prosecutor's speech about Secord's search for personal gain had sentenced him lightly. There was no reason to think he wouldn't be light with me too, but reason was not the governing factor. I *could* be sentenced to jail the next day; how many people could make that statement?

FRIDAY, NOVEMBER 15

Sentencing

I had slept reasonably well, considering. The kids were off from school, for a teachers' conference day, and my mother-in-law stayed with them while my wife, my father-in-law, and I went to court.

I was nervous. I tried not to think about what would happen next, in an hour or two, and I read the papers and a chapter in a biography of Churchill I was reading. Good escapism. At nine we left for the Courthouse, picking up Pierson on the way.

As I had been during my arraignment, I was once again numb in the courtroom. I was steeling myself for a jail term. Not that I expected it—I did not—but because it was, after all, theoretically possible, and I didn't want to be collapsing on the courtroom floor if it came. I told myself not to be unhappy with a McFarlane sentence, $20,000 in fines and two hundred hours community service.

And as I had been during my arraignment, I was once again trying to appear at ease. The press was out in force, and I did not want any reporters saying I was shaky.

Gregory Hunt seemed relaxed and happy, which I should have

201

taken as a hint that all was well. I didn't even notice when the prosecutors came in, led by Gillen—Walsh did not show—and was surprised when I looked up and they were there.

Shortly after 10 A.M., Judge Robinson entered the courtroom.

PROCEEDINGS

(Call to Order of the Court)

(Defendant Present)

THE COURT: Good morning.

THE CLERK: Criminal number 91-575, the United States versus Elliott Abrams. For the Government, Mr. Gillen; for the defendant, Mr. Pierson.

THE COURT: Mr. Pierson, will you and Mr. Abrams come forward, please.

The defendant Elliott Abrams is before the Court for sentencing, having been convicted after entering a plea to an information charging violation on two counts of Section 192 of Title 2 of the United States Code.

Is that correct?

MR. PIERSON: Yes, Your Honor.

THE COURT: All right. I will hear from you, Mr. Pierson.

MR. PIERSON: Your Honor, we have given the Court a filing with information as to the factors that we hope Your Honor will consider in passing sentence on Mr. Abrams, and you have also received a number of letters from Mr. Abrams' friends and colleagues, so I will speak only briefly.

THE COURT: You have all the time you would like, Mr. Pierson.

MR. PIERSON: Thank you, Your Honor. Your Honor, I want to say that this man, Elliott Abrams, is a decent and honorable man. He has spent most of his adult life in public service, by his choice. During that service, he has spent many years of working for human rights and for the development of democratic systems of government around the world—not just in Latin America, but in Europe and in Asia and in Africa.

And I hope that these good deeds to many people, including the people who wrote you to tell you about those deeds, will count for something in your passing judgment on Mr. Abrams today.

Mr. Abrams made a mistake, and he takes responsibility for that mistake; but it was not an effort to achieve personal, financial gain, and it was not a pattern of criminal conduct.

It was an isolated error in judgment, and we ask that you consider that error in the context of the more than a decade of Mr. Abrams' public service. Your Honor, I am an advocate, and you are entitled to consider my remarks in that context. You have heard from Mr. Abrams' friends and his colleagues in government, as well; and perhaps most important of all, you have heard via the presentence report from the probation officer who considered these matters.

And I would simply note the concluding sentence in that report, because it says more eloquently than I can what I believe the circumstances of this matter are. He says, "Mr. Abrams has paid a tremendous price, both personally and professionally; and it is unfortunate that his distinguished career in public service has been blemished by what appears to be a momentary lapse in judgment."

Your Honor, I ask that under the circumstances, you use the discretion that you have to suspend the imposition of a sentence and to place Mr. Abrams on probation. I earnestly suggest that such a course would be in the best interest of justice.

Thank you.

THE COURT: Mr. Abrams, what, if anything, would you like to say?

THE DEFENDANT: Your Honor, I think I would only— you've heard from Mr. Pierson and have his letter. I think I would only add that I would ask you, please, to take into account in the sentencing, not only the offenses that bring me here today, but as well the 12 years of service to the United States that preceded them and followed them.

Thank you.

THE COURT: All right. Would you have a seat, and I will hear from—Mr. Gillen, do you wish to elocute?

MR. GILLEN: Very briefly, Your Honor. As the Court is aware, pursuant to the agreement, we are to notify the Court of the cooperation of Mr. Abrams. He has cooperated with us. He has reviewed documents, voluminous amounts of documents. He has reviewed prior statements that he has made. He has granted us interviews, and he has done other matters that we have requested of him, pursuant to his plea agreement.

But I also would like to add that Mr. Abrams has conducted

himself in dealing with our office in a very professional manner—a manner that has impressed our office during what must have been surely troubling and difficult times for him. So, I would only add that, yes, Your Honor, he has fulfilled his cooperation with us.

Thank you.

THE COURT: Well, as you know, and the defendant knows, the offenses to which he entered his plea occurred before we were constrained by the new sentencing Act. So, therefore, as a federal judge, I'm entitled to use my judgment and discretion and can take into full consideration all of the evidence that relates to him as a person, as well as the evidence that relates to the activities involved.

And this is discretion that we cherish, that we exercise very carefully, and we regret that we no longer have; because much of what appears in the letters that have been received by the Court—and they come from some very distinguished people—much that we have heard from counsel, much that the probation officer has reported to the Court, as well as what Independent Counsel has said, would carry little weight under the present sentencing structure.

And I have read and reread the pre-sentence report and all the material, and I am of firm conviction that the appropriate sentence in this case doesn't require incarceration. So, would you come up, and you can come, too, Mr. Pierson, if you'd like.

Now, having been convicted by your plea to the counts of violation of Section 192, Title 2 of the United States Code, it's the judgment of this Court that the imposition of sentence be suspended; that you be placed on probation for two years.

I am required by the law to impose a $25.00 assessment for each count of the information to which you entered your plea. And I'm also going to require that you contribute 100 hours of community service, because I believe that there are those, especially in your profession, who could gain from your experience; and to that end I would encourage the probation office to work with you in some fashion to make known to other lawyers the fact that there will be occasions in their professional life when they must rely at bottom upon the oath they took when they became members of a Bar.

And I think there are some ethical considerations that you have experienced that could be well brought to the attention of some of the younger members of our Bar—and perhaps some of the older members. So, I am suggesting that you have a contribution that I think the legal community at least should have the value of. Whether the community at large appreciates it or not is not my concern at the moment.

So, that's why I'm imposing the 100 hours of community service. Our past experience has been, when we have had the necessity of working with people who find themselves in the position which you now find, that they have made substantial contributions, very significant in ways that would surprise the larger community, but in ways that have been very helpful to the people that we serve, who get themselves involved in the criminal system as we attempt to rehabilitate lives.

I am not suggesting that your life needs rehabilitating. I am suggesting rather, that you have a contribution that we would like to have the benefit of with respect to others that we are forced to work with. Now, if you don't understand me, I think Mr. Hunt, the probation officer will. He's an experienced probation officer. He's worked with us for a long time. He understands me, as most people do who hang around long enough.

But that's it; that's my judgment. That's the judgment of the Court; that's the judgment that will be entered as of this date.

And Mr. Hunt will tell you what he wants you to do and when.

MR. PIERSON: Thank you, Your Honor.

THE COURT: Very Well.

(Whereupon, the hearing was concluded at 10:15 A.M.)

The judge had been remarkably kind in his tone, in his "body language," in his words. He had given Pierson "all the time you need," but asked Gillen if he wished "to elocute." He had gone out of his way to say nice things, and to say them nicely.

Clearly the letters he had received had impressed him, and they were impressive indeed. Some lawyers are cynical about these things, suggesting that judges don't ever bother to read the letters so painstakingly gathered for them. But here they seemed to have made a huge difference.

And he had imposed no fine, no fine at all, just the fifty dollars court costs the law required him to charge me. The only "penalty" he had imposed was one hundred hours of community service, and in describing it he had, again, been very kind. "There are those, especially in your profession, who could gain from your experience," the judge had said; "you have a contribution that we would like to have the benefit of," dealing with ethical considerations lawyers and officials face.

This felt like vindication. I turned around and saw there were tears of relief and happiness on Rachel's face. We embraced. Rachel and DeVier embraced. Peter Morgan and Barry Levine were there in court, too, and we all embraced as well.

Walsh. What can he have thought, I wondered. The very same day, one floor above me in the Courthouse, the Court of Appeals threw out the Poindexter conviction, just as had happened in the North case. So what had Walsh achieved with his five years and fifty million dollars? The cases he had tried, North and Poindexter, he had lost. The cases he had gotten pleas on, like mine, had been more or less tossed out by judges. So the judicial system was saying, go home!

What goes through your mind as you stand there, waiting to be sentenced? I recall staring, while Pierson spoke, first at the Great Seal of the Republic, carved in gold into the marble wall behind the judge, and then at the flag by his side. I remembered Secretary Shultz's story, told to many foreign presidents during my years with him, of why the eagle faced the olive branches rather than the arrows. Initially it had faced the arrows, but Truman had turned it around for obvious symbolic reasons. I recall thinking, what if I fell down, right here and now? Who would be the first to pick me up? I recall wondering if my expression, my posture, would "count" as the judge made up his mind. And I recall that when he leaned forward and wrote something, I wondered if he had added to or stricken some part of the sentence.

After the sentencing, I remained numb. It was great news, of course, but I did not actually feel elated. I still felt disoriented. As I said to Rachel, I felt like a visitor from another planet, and I wanted to ask, "Who set up *this* trip?" I was at first a little annoyed about Poindexter, for he would get off scot-free, I thought, without any criminal record, as had North, while I would have one. But that feeling lasted only a moment, for I could imagine—now, I truly could imagine—what he had been through. He had been through five years of it and had stood before a federal judge who had sentenced him to prison.

I would not trade places with him. It amazed me that I had even momentarily thought to myself, he got off scot-free. He had paid a huge price.

After the sentencing I went with Hunt to his office, and he read me the rules. I would appear the following week for an orientation session on community service and on probation, and then meet with my probation officer—who would not be he. I was sorry for that, for he was a fair man and I had looked forward to continuing to see him.

The probation rules were no joke. "You shall not leave the judicial district without permission of the court or probation officer." Hunt explained this was interpreted to mean suburban Virginia and Maryland were okay, but any farther trips—to see my mother in New York, I realized, or to take the kids to the beach—required permission. Foreign travel? For that you needed the court's permission, which could take three or four weeks.

"You shall report to the probation officer . . . and shall submit a truthful and complete written report within the first five days of each month." The reporting form included not only unchanging data (address, employment, cars owned) but financial data ("net income from employment—attach proof of earnings; total monthly income; total monthly expenses; bank balance, checking and savings"). Then it asked, "List all purchases of individual goods or services for which you paid $500 or more."

Oops. One question was "Did you have any contact with anyone having a criminal record?" Gee, I thought, half of my former colleagues now had a criminal record.

The probation rules continued: Follow these rules. Support your family. Notify the probation officer re any change in residence or employment. Refrain from excessive use of alcohol. Do not use drugs. Do not associate with any person convicted of a felony. Then a more curious one: "You shall not enter into any agreement to act as an informer or a special agent of a law enforcement agency without the permission of the court." What? Why not? Well, I thought, that's someone else's problem. Mine will be to hire an accountant, I guessed.

The rules were, well, demeaning. Get permission to visit your mother. Tell us your income, your bank balance. File your reports. But

I did not blame the judge for that, or the Probation Service, for they hadn't done this to me; Walsh had. Gillen had been kind in Court, of course; he had said exactly what he had promised Pierson he would. One of my lawyers said, yeah, he saw the way the wind was blowing all right, and decided to try and get on the right side of it. I thought Gillen was perhaps abashed by the error he had made and Pierson's anger at him for this. And maybe now, when it was all over, he had had a moment of doubt and had wondered if pursuing me had actually served "justice." Who could say?

Anyway, I was no less furious at all of them. To say that the judge had done all he could to limit the damage to me, to say that he had acknowledged what I had done in twelve years in government, was to say nothing about Walsh and Gillen, who had insisted, absolutely insisted, that I have a criminal record. What a wonderful achievement for five years and fifty million dollars. I wondered what Judge Robinson made of it all, when he pondered their record in his chambers.

When we finished with Hunt, we went outside to meet the press and I read my statement:

> I want to express my gratitude to Chief Judge Robinson and Gregory Hunt of the US Probation Service for the fairness they have shown me today and over the last several weeks.
>
> This is not the occasion for me to talk about this case. As I said on October 7th, I take full responsibility for my actions and for my testimony in October, 1986. I believe this case does raise some serious and important public policy issues, and in due course I plan to address those.
>
> I'd like to thank the many colleagues and former colleagues, friends, and other Americans who have come forward in the past weeks to offer me and my family their support. I'm very proud of that support, and proud of the contribution I made in twelve years of service to the United States Government.
>
> I'm glad to put this matter behind me, and get back to work.

JUDGMENTS

Getting back to work does not mean getting back to normal, I found out. There were legal bills to pay, and therefore funds to raise; there were thank-yous Rachel and I owed to so many friends, and for that matter strangers, who had stood with us; and there was probation and my hundred hours of community service.

The dread that had pervaded my life since 1986 was now gone. For the first time in five years I could go to sleep at night knowing that lawyers and FBI agents were no longer poring over my words and looking for a way to get me. I was free of Walsh and his boys forever. I found I did not miss them.

But the passage of time has not cooled my anger. What happened to me should never have happened in this country. Lawrence Walsh should be the last man ever empowered to turn political disputes into crimes.

A Separate and Unequal System of Justice

For most American citizens, the federal criminal justice system is filled with safeguards. First, there must be a crime committed, setting the whole machine in motion. Next, a U.S. Attorney must try to determine who has committed it. An individual will not be named, and his reputation thereby damaged, until a formal decision has been made to charge him with a crime. Finally, if someone is charged with the crime, his trial will revolve around the question of his culpability. The defendant asserts his innocence, the government must prove his guilt, and they're off.

Of course, it may never get that far. The U.S. Attorney may decide not to prosecute for many reasons. He may decide it is unfair to pursue one defendant while others who were clearly involved remain unindicted. He may view the alleged violation as technical rather than substantial, and not worth pursuing. He may believe there was no criminal intent. He may feel the case is unimportant, preferring to use his resources for more serious cases.

The legal system established by Congress to pursue senior officials of the Executive Branch bears no resemblance to this at all.

Under the so-called Ethics in Government Act (28 USCA 591-599), it is Congress, not a U.S. Attorney, who most often selects the victim. The mechanism starts its whirring when the Judiciary Committee of either House of Congress—or a majority of either Committee's Democrats or Republicans—demands that the Attorney General agree to the appointment of an "Independent Counsel" to investigate the activities of certain Administration officials. On occasion officials have themselves requested the appointment of an independent counsel, but this occurs when congressional pressure is enormous and the official wishes to head them off at the pass and appear cooperative. The Attorney General can refuse only if he is able to certify that "there are *no* reasonable grounds to believe that further investigation is warranted." But he is unable to conduct such an investigation himself: the Ethics in Government Act limits his time and forbids him to issue subpoenas, convene a grand jury, or use the usual investigative tools. With his hands so tied, he is virtually forced to agree. How can he prove the negative? How can he state flatly that there has been no crime committed, that there was no criminal intent, that there are *no* grounds for further investigation?

Thus, in any controversial matter, it is clear what will happen, and has happened: when Congress demands an Independent Counsel, it gets one. But notice what has transpired here: Congress has not said, "A crime may have been committed. Find a culprit." It has said, "Here are some possible culprits. Find a crime." It has done damage to people's reputations even before a prosecutor has come on the scene.

Now, who is given this task of finding a crime to fit the culprits? Neither the Justice Department nor any of the U.S. Attorneys around the country can be involved. The Ethics in Government Act establishes a new court as a division of the U.S. Court of Appeals in Washington, calling it the "Special Division," and its one and only responsibility is the appointment and supervision of Independent Counsels. The President and the Attorney General have no say in the matter at all.

But the Independent Counsel is just one person. He will need a staff, maybe even a big staff. Where does it come from? He has complete discretion in this. Given the situation, he will choose lawyers who are willing to drop whatever they are doing, to suspend their own careers, to leave their families behind, to come to Washington for an indeterminate number of months or years. The only thing they can be sure of is this: they are coming to investigate and perhaps prosecute the President or some of his top aides, people who have been picked out in advance by Congress.

What kind of lawyer will volunteer for this? Is he likely to be a lawyer sympathetic to the President and his policies? A lawyer of absolute fair-mindedness, without any bias against the Administration? A lawyer who believes it is possible that *no* crime has been committed, who truly affords the accused the presumption of innocence, who looks forward to packing his bag and going quietly home after a couple of months?

Not likely, and in the main not so. The Independent Counsel's staff is inevitably a beehive of bias, buzzing with prejudgments, prejudices, and political partiality. Supreme Court Justice Scalia wrote "the prospect is frightening" (*Morrison* v. *Olson,* 108 S. Ct. 2597, 2630 [1988]); I can tell him, the reality is too.

The best proof of this bias can be found in a revealing interview Lawrence Walsh himself gave to *The Washington Times*. Walsh was asked about the things his former staff member Jeffrey Toobin had written, criticizing excessive use of the criminal process and acknowledging that despite the desire to prosecute me they simply hadn't had adequate evidence against me. Walsh's comment about Toobin was candid, if shocking: "He missed his target. He was supposed to get Abrams. We hit the target after he left." So much for fairness, so much for justice: "He was supposed to get Abrams."

What are the restraints, the limits, under which this new Independent Counsel and his staff will work? There are no financial restraints, for Congress writes blank checks for his operation. He has no other cases, no competing interests; therefore nothing takes too much time or money or manpower, no issue is too small, no infraction "merely technical." What about guidelines? The "Independent" Counsel, though entirely dependent on Congress, is independent of the Justice Department and the President. He follows Justice's rules as he sees fit, ignoring them when he finds them too constraining. While the statute calls on him to follow Justice Department policies, that provision is a dead letter: he is the sole judge of whether and when to do so, and there are no sanctions to enforce his compliance. As for precedents, there are none, for each successive Independent Counsel is new, as is his staff, and there is precious little case law applicable to their work. In its 1975 report, the Watergate Special Prosecution Force warned against the establishment of a permanent office of special prosecutor, independent from the Justice Department, because a "relatively small group of persons falling within a permanent special prosecutor's jurisdiction could be subject to a much heavier hammer of Federal criminal law than the rest of the nation which is subject to Department of Justice standards." It is now very clear that this warning was prescient.

What if the Independent Counsel seems to be going off the track, engaging in prosecutorial behavior that no U.S. Attorney's office would countenance? Can the Justice Department be appealed to? No, for it may not supervise the Independent Counsel's work. Can the Attorney General or President fire him? Not really, for the Ethics in Government Act says he can be fired only for "good cause," a phrase meant to restrict the President's power so narrowly that he may act only in response to malfeasance. An appeal to that Special Division, the new court, is likely to be unavailing, for it has no written rules of procedure whatsoever. What is more, the Independent Counsel will already have established a relationship with that court, which after all has expressed its confidence in him by appointing him in the first place.

In 1940, before becoming a Supreme Court Justice, Attorney General Robert Jackson delivered a speech to a gathering of U.S. Attorneys. I have noted a part of this address earlier, but it is worth quoting a bit more now:

> Law enforcement is not automatic. It isn't blind. One of the greatest difficulties of the position of prosecutor is that he must pick his cases, because no prosecutor can ever investigate all of the cases in which he receives complaints. . . . If the prosecutor is obliged to choose his cases, it follows that he can choose his defendants. Therein is the most dangerous power of the prosecutor: that he will pick people that he thinks he should get, rather than cases that need to be prosecuted. With the law books filled with a great assortment of crimes, a prosecutor stands a fair chance of finding at least a technical violation of some act on the part of almost anyone . . . it is not a question of discovering the commission of a crime . . . it is a question of picking the man and then . . . pin[ning] some offense on him. It is in this realm . . . that the greatest danger of abuse of prosecuting power lies. It is here that law enforcement becomes personal. [Robert Jackson, "The Federal Prosecutor," address delivered at the Second Annual Conference of United States Attorneys, April 1, 1940]

Fifty years ago Jackson worried that a busy prosecutor would pick "people he thinks he should get"; he could not even envision a day when Congress would take that task upon itself and establish a separate prosecutorial system dedicated solely to pursuing those victims. Can there be any doubt that he, like Justice Scalia, would have called the Independent Counsel system "frightening"?

A Government of Men, Not Laws

Most Americans have heard and understood the phrase, "a government of laws, and not of men." When it comes to criminal law in particular, citizens are supposed to be governed by carefully defined statutes. The idea is that the citizen has the right to know, in advance, what constitutes criminal conduct and what does not. If the law has been unclear, the Supreme Court has always construed it very narrowly, giving the citizen the benefit of the doubt. As the U.S. Court of Appeals said recently, "a penal statute must define the criminal offense with sufficient definiteness that ordinary people can understand what conduct it prohibits, and do so in a manner that does not invite arbitrary and discriminatory enforcement" (*United States* v. *Poindexter,* 951 F. 2d. 369, 378 [D.C. Cir. 1991]). Article I of the Constitution specifically bars any "bill of attainder or ex post facto law" which would turn a heretofore lawful act into a crime.

But in the hands of the Independent Counsel, the law is subject to change at any time, and it is impossible to discern what is legal and what is not.

Ought congressional testimony by Executive Branch officials to be judged as if it were given in a court of law, or by the broader boundaries of political speech? For two centuries the answer was clearly the latter.

For two centuries Executive Branch witnesses were free to advocate their President's policies—short of outright perjury—without the risk of jail. But those fluid political standards do not apply whenever Congress decides, in an act of political pique over policies it doesn't like, to change the rules. This can be done in a flash and held retroactively against officials who have had no reason to dream of facing this grim outcome.

But what is the new rule? In brief, it is: *Testify at your peril when Congress is angry.* Could a President be prosecuted for misleading Congress in his State of the Union message? Can an official be prosecuted for something said in a press release or press conference? What about a campaign speech? What kinds of "withholding information" are criminal, and what kinds are not? Can anyone tell a new official what the guidelines are? Does anyone who watched the Gates and Thomas hearings believe a *legal* standard can be deduced from those?

No one knows. That is the truth, and that is why prosecuting people for such "crimes" is so foreign to American justice. It is a triple whammy Administration officials face: first is the floating standard—sometimes loose enough to allow most "political" speech, and sometimes as tough as the courtroom standard of absolute accuracy. Second is the difficulty of predicting which standard will be applied, for the decision is made after the fact. Third is the fact that the decision to prosecute is in effect made by Congress, on a case-by-case, witness-by-witness basis. Whatever that is, it is not justice.

Let us say for example that the President has privately decided to announce in his State of the Union address that he will ask Congress to lower taxes. There's no written decision, but he has told his Secretary of the Treasury over a drink that that's what he's going to do. He has also said, "Mum's the word. Let's make this a surprise." The Secretary goes up to the Hill and is asked, "Mr. Secretary, I believe the President has already decided to ask us to lower taxes. Isn't that right?" The Secretary replies, "No formal decision has been made." The Senator asks, "Oh, sure, but the decision really has been made, hasn't it, Mr. Secretary? Be honest with us." He answers, "No, Senator, there's no formal decision."

Withholding information from Congress? False testimony? In truth no one can say, given the state of the law today. Put this testimony into the context of some bitter dispute, and there's no reason why that Senator could not listen to the State of the Union address, hear the President say he was going to ask Congress to lower taxes, and immediately call for an Independent Counsel to investigate.

When did the President decide? What is a "formal" decision? What and when did he tell the Secretary? What did the Secretary's notes say? How many drafts were there of his testimony, and what did he tell the staff members who drafted it? Did he say, Look, the President has decided this, but we're not going to say that? Such an inquiry is no longer out of bounds. It needs only an angry Representative or Senator to get it going. The Secretary might never hear about it again, or he could be hounded for years by an Independent Counsel determined to prove that he committed some crime.

In January 1989, as the Reagan Administration was ending and I was leaving the government, I received a booklet describing new laws governing conflicts of interest for former officials. Congress had held hearings and had debated several drafts, and the President had signed into law a bill calling for a two-year "cooling off" period. During this time former officials were enjoined from lobbying the agency where they had worked. Fair enough, I thought. There was a new law, properly enacted by Congress and approved by the President, whose terms very clearly explained what was required, and you knew where you stood.

Such clear standards emerging from carefully drawn statutes do not confine the Independent Counsel's search for tainted testimony. He may therefore come at you five years after the fact and say, "Here are the standards! Plead guilty or go to trial!" Unspoken is the whole truth: "Here are the standards! We've just invented them, and how dare you not to have complied in 1985!"

As the Red Queen said in *Alice in Wonderland*, "Sentence first, verdict after."

United States *v.* Abrams: *Another Look*

I pleaded guilty, as I said on page one of this book, to two counts of withholding information from Congress. It is worth turning back again to those counts, to see precisely what conduct it was that the Independent Counsel insisted on criminalizing.

Count One against me related to testimony given on October 10, 1986, to the Senate Foreign Relations Committee in the aftermath of the shoot-down of a Contra supply flight on October 5, and the Sandinista capture of Eugene Hasenfus. Obviously, I knew, as everyone knew, that the Administration wholeheartedly approved of these flights and of all the private activities in aid of the Contras. I did not know that Oliver North, or any other U.S. Government official, was exercising operational control over that network or violating any law, including the Boland Amendment. In fact, North had assured me and my colleagues that he was *not* violating any law, and that he had checked this with the White House lawyers. After the shoot-down, there was much speculation that the U.S. Government had been involved in the flight, but I believed this to be false. I had checked with the U.S. Embassy in El Salvador (the country from which the plane had taken off), the National Security Council, the Defense Department, and the CIA, and had never been told of any U.S. Government role. On the basis of these assurances, I told Secretary Shultz, and he, the President, and I made public statements to the effect that the U.S. Government had not been involved in the Hasenfus flight. I made those statements on October 5, 6, 7, 8, and 9, and again to the Committee on October 10. At no time— -during those days, or in the weeks after—did any U.S. Government official, from any agency, contradict me or suggest to me that my denials were wrong or were too categorical.

In the October 10 testimony, I was asked about a *Los Angeles Times* article that had appeared that morning, reporting an elaborate system of private support for the Contras and alleging that U.S. officials had assumed a central role in running it, in violation of the Boland Amendment. I answered this way:

> In the last two years, since Congress cut off support to the Resistance, this supply system has kept them alive. It is not our supply system. It is one that grew up after we were forbidden from supplying the Resistance, and we have been kind of careful not to get closely involved with it and to stay away from it. . . .

> I think that people who are supplying the Contras believe that we generally approve of what they are doing—and they are right. We do generally approve of what they are doing, because they are keeping the Contras alive while Congress makes its decision, which each House has separately, though obviously final legislation is not yet ready.

> So, the notion that we are generally in favor of people helping the Contras is correct.

> We do not encourage people to do this. We don't round up people, we don't write letters, we don't have conversations, we don't tell them to do this, we don't ask them to do it. But I think it is quite clear, from the attitude of the Administration, the attitude of the Administration is that these people are doing a very good thing, and if they think they are doing something that we like, then, in a general sense, they are right. But that is without any encouragement and coordination from us, other than a public speech by the President, that kind of thing, on the public record.

I was not trying, in this answer, to deny the evident and lawful contacts between the Administration and private individuals helping the Contras; I had met some of them myself in the Roosevelt Room of the White House. Rather, I was trying here to refute the central allegation of the article, which I believed to be false: namely, that there was U.S. Government involvement in assembling or operating the private supply network. It bears noting that my words were not part of any prepared text but were a spontaneous response to an unexpected question about an article that had just appeared.

The Independent Counsel also knew the next act in the drama. On the evening of October 23, a CIA official gave me some information that indicated there might be a link between the CIA's Station Chief in San José, Costa Rica, and Oliver North. Shaken by this disclosure, I took it to Secretary Shultz's top staff at 7 A.M. the following day and said I needed to see the Secretary immediately. Shultz's staff took notes of my meeting with him, and the Independent Counsel has them. They show me briefing Shultz on what I had just learned and saying "the CIA is involved in these flights—after I have been out there for two weeks saying absolutely not. . . . Ollie assures me he has talked to White House counsel and is not doing anything illegal."

Besides showing what I knew and did not know, these notes show how I acted when I thought there might be a violation of law or received important new information. It is worth adding that neither the Secretary nor his staff felt that we should rush back to the Hill, or make public statements, withdrawing any past assurances that had been given. We did not really know what the facts were. We were being told the CIA's Inspector General would be investigating. In the meantime we would maintain silence.

The Independent Counsel, in the Information that substitutes for an indictment in plea agreement cases, said that on October 10 I "knew that Lt. Col. North had been in contact with people supplying the Contras, had conversations with people supplying the Contras, and had asked and encouraged them to supply the Contras." The issue here is not whether I withheld *any* information from Congress, for by my plea agreement I acknowledged that. The issue is whether *under any normal standards,* under the standards applied to testimony on policy issues for two centuries, my testimony should have led to a criminal prosecution. I submit that the very clear answer is *no*.

Count Two is, if anything, even weaker. In December 1985, Congress expressly modified the Boland Amendment to confirm the authority of the State Department to solicit funds from foreign governments for aid to the Contras. At a May 1986 meeting President Reagan decided that the United States should approach one or more foreign governments, and I was assigned the task of coming up with candidates. After canvassing several of my colleagues, I suggested Brunei as a likely prospect, and that suggestion was approved. In a subsequent trip to Southeast Asia, Secretary Shultz visited Brunei and mentioned the Central America situation to the Sultan. On the Secretary's return, the Department made arrangements, via the U.S. Embassy in Brunei, for a U.S. Government representative to speak with an official of the Sultan's government and make the solicitation, and I was designated to be that U.S. representative. In August 1986 I visited London and asked the Sultan's aide for that support, and in late August we were advised by the U.S. Embassy in Brunei that the request had been approved. This request was in all respects lawful—this solicitation was fully authorized by the President and the Secretary of State, and State Department solicitation of humanitarian aid for the Contras was permitted by Congress in Section 105(b)(2) of the Intelligence Authorization Act for Fiscal Year 1986 (PL 99-169)—but it was regarded as an extremely sensitive diplomatic undertaking. The Government of Brunei had asked for, and had received, our assurance of total secrecy, and extraordinary measures were taken in the Department to prevent any spread of the knowledge.

The money never arrived in any Contra or Contra-related account, because, as we later learned, a clerical error had been made in the transcribing of the account number.

On October 14, 1986, testifying before the House Permanent Select Committee on Intelligence, I was asked, "Do you know if any foreign government is helping to supply the Contras? There is a report in the LA paper, for example, that the Saudis are." I answered that the "story about the Saudis to my knowledge is false," a statement I believed at that time to be true. No one in the Independent Counsel's office ever asserted that I had any knowledge of the super-secret Saudi contributions. I was then asked, "Is it also false with respect to other governments as well?" and I responded, "Yes, it is also false."

Obviously, this statement withheld from the Committee the solicitation of Brunei, for I did not believe I was at liberty to disclose it. As Secretary Shultz wrote to a number of congressmen in 1987, "At the time Mr. Abrams gave his testimony, we had given that country a pledge of absolute confidentiality and Mr. Abrams felt properly bound by that pledge." Moreover, I did not say we had never made a solicitation or received a promise: I said no foreign government was helping the Contras, because we had not yet received a dime from Brunei. Whatever the Contras were living on, I was confident, it was not money from Brunei or any other foreign government, and it was therefore accurate to say no foreign government at that time "was helping."

There was another act to this drama, too. I gave similar testimony, withholding information about the Brunei solicitation, to the Senate Intelligence Committee on November 25, 1986. But that was the day the Iran/Contra affair broke, the day Attorney General Meese held a press conference announcing that there had been arms sales to Iran and that some of the proceeds had been diverted to the Contras. Just hours after the Meese announcement, I went up to testify at a previously scheduled meeting of the committee and, when asked about foreign government help, gave the same answer: none. No money from Brunei had arrived, and indeed by then I was wondering if it ever would, so I gave the same answer I had given on October 14.

But I realized the informal rules governing relations with Congress might be changing now, for Washington was in a major political crisis. I was unhappy with my failure to tell the committee about Brunei, and upon returning to the Department I asked for permission to tell the committee about the solicitation. Secretary Shultz was traveling, and Thanksgiving then intervened, but as soon as he gave me permission I informed the committee. This is no doubt why the Independent Counsel did *not* charge me with withholding information from the Senate Intelligence Committee: I cured the problem as soon as I could.

Still, Walsh insisted on charging me with withholding information on October 14. As with Count One, the issue here is not whether I withheld *any* information from Congress, for by my plea agreement I acknowledged that. The issue, as with Count One, is whether *under any normal standards,* under the standards applied to testimony on policy issues for two centuries, my testimony should have led to a criminal prosecution. Once again I submit that the very clear answer is *no.*

What are, or what historically have been, "normal standards"? Peter Morgan has given a few answers in an article he published in the Winter 1992 edition of *Northwestern University Law Review* (vol. 86, no. 2, p. 177) entitled "The Undefined Crime of Lying to Congress: Ethics Reform and the Rule of Law."

Morgan begins with statements made to Congress by President James Polk in 1846 concerning the Mexican War. Here Polk falsely blamed the onset of hostilities on Mexico, and falsely claimed he had no desire to take any Mexican territory. There were widespread assertions that Polk had lied to Congress. In January 1848 Representative Abraham Lincoln voted for a resolution claiming that the war had been "unnecessarily and unconstitutionally commenced by the President" and called for a congressional inquiry. When the Senate ratified the peace treaty of Guadalupe Hidalgo in March 1848, however, the issue was quickly dropped.

Jumping a century ahead to 1958, Morgan discusses the CIA's intervention in Indonesia. The Agency was assisting antigovernment rebels in that country, and in May of that year a CIA-sponsored bomber was shot down and its American pilot captured. Secretary of State Dulles promptly testified to the House Foreign Affairs Committee that the United States was not violating international law and not intervening in Indonesia's internal affairs. President Eisenhower affirmed this, saying we were not taking sides in Indonesia and were being carefully neutral. Days later the Indonesian government presented the captured pilot and his documents, which linked him to the U.S. Government. No one in Congress called for an investigation of Dulles's testimony—or of Eisenhower's misleading statements, for that matter.

Six years later, Morgan tells us, in August 1964, the Johnson Administration misled Congress about the origins of the Gulf of Tonkin incident, in which North Vietnamese patrol boats had attacked an

American ship. In fact, the U.S. Navy and South Vietnamese ships had engaged in a series of attacks on North Vietnam prior to the incident, and there had already been some shooting incidents involving American ships. But Secretary of Defense McNamara told a special joint meeting of the Senate Armed Services and Foreign Relations Committees: "Our Navy played absolutely no role in, was not associated with, was not aware of, any South Vietnamese action, if there were any." Neither then nor later was there any congressional inquiry into McNamara's testimony, which Morgan covers in a section entitled "McNamara's False Statement."

And lest the Johnson Administration be considered unusually mendacious, it is worth mentioning an incident from the Kennedy years not recorded by Morgan. Writing in his memoirs, *Danger and Survival,* (New York, 1988), McGeorge Bundy, President Kennedy's National Security Adviser, gives an interesting account of actions taken by that Administration over the Cuban missile crisis of 1962. The Soviets had put missiles into Cuba, and Kennedy was insistent that they be removed. He decided to inform Khrushchev as part of a solution to this crisis that America's Jupiter missiles would be removed from Turkey. In an Oval Office meeting on October 27, 1962, Kennedy and his senior advisers "agreed without hesitation that no one not in the room was to be informed" of the message to Khrushchev conveying this decision. Bundy argues that this secret assurance to Khrushchev and the "collateral" deception that accompanied it were justified by overwhelming national interests. But he admits that by "keeping to ourselves the assurance on the Jupiters, we misled our colleagues, our countrymen, our successors, and our allies."

Not to mention Congress. Secretary of Defense McNamara was asked at a House hearing, "Are you aware of any agreement, any assurance . . . to Khrushhev that if he would withdraw at the time under the conditions you showed us, the United States would thereby commit itself to any particular course of action?" It was a sensitive question, for there had been some Republican suspicion of a secret deal. McNamara did not duck. He simply replied: "I am not only unaware of any agreement, it is inconceivable to me that our President would enter into a discussion of any such agreement. Moreover, there were absolutely no undisclosed agreements associated with the with-drawal of Soviet missiles from Cuba.'' No action was ever taken against McNamara for this testimony.

Examples from other Administrations could also be taken, but the point is clear enough. From the last century right up until recent years, witnesses had extraordinary leeway in policy communications to Congress. The testimony I gave in 1986 would have been considered miles within the borders of trouble, and it would have been laughable to suggest that it was criminal.

Congress and the Executive at War

Why all this has changed recently is not mysterious. The conflict between the Executive and Legislative branches is built into our Constitution, and is one of the bulwarks of our liberty. The advent of political parties did not harm that old interbranch rivalry or embitter it, for each party understood that it might at one time control the Presidency and at another the Congress. The rights of both branches were protected. But in recent years, the Republicans have had a virtually uninterrupted tenure in the White House, while the Democrats have controlled the Congress, and that once healthy interbranch rivalry has been permeated with poison.

As the Republican Presidents have generally come from the conservative wing of their party, while the Democrats who control their party's caucus in Congress are from their party's Left, even the familiar interparty rivalry is now infected with a special Left–Right bitterness that is relatively new.

The result is an often vicious power struggle between Congress and the Executive Branch, and in this war the President's soldiers face very heavy artillery from the Hill. Indeed, in certain cases they face the prospect of being selected by Congress for investigation and prosecution by an Independent Counsel appointed for this precise purpose and responsive to Congress, not the President.

Needless to say, this changes the way every Presidential appointee must view that field of battle with Congress. After all, if you get them mad at you, will you face their angry speeches, their denunciations in the press, their calls for your resignation—*or a prosecutor?* Is it worth a criminal trial, with the endless time and expense? Judge Learned Hand gave a concise description of these effects in an opinion he wrote:

> [T]o submit all officials, the innocent as well as the guilty, to the burden of a trial and to the inevitable danger of its outcome, would dampen the ardor of all but the most resolute, or the most irresponsible, in the unflinching discharge of their duties. Again and again the public interest calls for action which may turn out to be founded on a mistake, in the face of which an official may later find himself hard put to it to satisfy a grand jury of his good faith. [*Gregoire* v. *Biddle,* 177 F. 2d. 579, 581 (2d Cir. 1949)]

The Founding Fathers were well aware of the dangers of political prosecutions and were determined to prevent one branch from using them against another. The danger they foresaw was that the President, who controlled prosecutions, would move against congressmen and Senators he disliked, as British Kings had used the law courts to intimidate and punish Members of Parliament. To this end they gave members of Congress absolute protection for their official duties in the "Speech and Debate Clause" of Article I of the Constitution. No lie, no slander, however vile, can be punished so long as it is made as part of official business—not because such acts are approved of, but because allowing the President or the courts to start prosecuting and trying members of Congress this way is a road without an end. Down it lie unacceptable risks to the independence of Congress.

The Founding Fathers did not supply similar protection to the courts, but many courts have given it to themselves, allowing traditional trial tactics to be pursued by witnesses and lawyers trying to win a case.

Only the Executive Branch, the President and his staff, were not provided this protection, and it is easy to see why: if they were doing the prosecuting, they could protect themselves. If there were a complaint, Executive Branch officials likely to be sympathetic to the problems another official faced would decide whether to prosecute. If there were an argument about not divulging secrets in the trial or harming national security by undertaking the prosecution, or a claim that this particular prosecution was unwise or unfair, it would get a fair hearing.

So it used to be. Today, the normal criminal justice system that governs the lives of other Americans no longer applies to Executive Branch officials at odds with members of Congress. The decision to prosecute, and the conduct of the prosecution, can lie well beyond the control or even the influence of the Executive Branch. Thus, while the ability of the President to protect his subordinates is greatly reduced, the power of Congress vis-à-vis the Presidency is greatly enhanced.

The Congress can fight the Executive Branch politically, with the tools the Constitution provides. It can launch a major investigation of its own. It can refuse to vote any money for the agency whose officials it is angry at, or for some pet projects of the President. It can refuse to allow the officials, or their superiors, to testify. It can tie up other important legislation, thereby tying the Administration in knots. Ultimately, according to the Constitution, it can impeach any "civil officer" serving in the Administration.

These traditional political remedies give the Congress immense power, and they are fair and constitutional. But the current system, in which congressionally selected victims for criminal trials face standards that may shift with every passing political wind, has stretched the notion of political remedy very far indeed. Though the Supreme Court ruled it constitutional in 1988 (notwithstanding a brilliant dissent by Justice Scalia), it is—constitutional or not—deeply unfair. No American should ever be treated this way again.

Fixing the Independent Counsel's Office

There are some actions, any of which, if taken, could help to restore the system of justice to Americans. First and foremost would be to eliminate the Office of Independent Counsel entirely. By its terms, the Independent Counsel Reauthorization Act of 1987 lasts for five years only and will expire on December 15, 1992. On that day it should be permitted to die altogether. If Congress should choose to reauthorize the Independent Counsel system for yet another five years, the President, acting in the best interests of the citizens he serves, should exercise his veto power. This is what President Reagan should have done in 1982 and 1987, instead of signing the reauthorization legislation into law (acting, in 1987, against the recommendation of the Justice Department that he exercise a veto). After all, the Justice Department and the U.S. Attorneys have proved themselves, hundreds of times, quite capable of handling even the most sensitive cases. Moreover, Congress and the press have proved *themselves* just as capable of pushing and shoving at prosecutors to assure that they are diligent and honest, without commencing the Spanish Inquisition.

If Congress is unwilling to eliminate the whole concept, which is probable, and the President is unwilling to exercise a veto on *any* reauthorization, there are ways of making this institution less offensive and unfair. A new law could limit the reach of the Office of Independent Counsel to fewer officials—to those, say, at only the very highest levels: Cabinet members and the top handful of White House aides. Cases involving them are the most sensitive, where political interference is perhaps most to be feared.

Congress could change the statute so that the Justice Department's jurisdiction could be removed and an Independent Counsel appointed only after careful study had revealed positive evidence that Justice could *not* do a good and fair job in a given case.

The Attorney General could be permitted to conduct a full preliminary investigation of a case and to dismiss it if he determined that no crimes had been committed. This would eliminate the "prove the negative" standard that makes the appointment of an Independent Counsel a foregone conclusion.

If an Independent Counsel were appointed, Congress or the Justice Department, or that Special Court, could put a limit on its budget and its calendar, to ensure that it did not drag on into the next decade pursuing its victims.

Congress might impose some rules on the Office of Independent Counsel itself, and on the Special Division, so that defendants could understand the procedures and make certain their rights were fully protected.

If there is to be an Office of Independent Counsel, its jurisdiction should cover Congress as well as the Executive Branch. When members of Congress understand that they too may face the Star Chamber proceedings that have recently characterized the OIC, they are much more likely to think seriously about fairness and justice in the conduct of its activities.

And, finally, the Independent Counsel's report could be eliminated entirely. This is the position of the American Bar Association, which has said that people who have been investigated by the OIC "should not have their reputations damaged and their privacy invaded by disclosure of information that does not suffice to give rise to a criminal charge." ("Summary Report and Recommendations," Independent Counsel Subcommittee of the Criminal Justice Section of the ABA White Collar Crime Committee, August 19, 1989, at pp. 7–8.)

This report, issued by the Independent Counsel at the end of his term, summarizes his work. Here he has the opportunity to discuss at length, among other things, cases that were never brought to a disposition. Thus citizens never charged with any crime may be exposed to a kind of public hanging, without any recourse to a system of laws that might help them to restore their good names. Prosecutors have every opportunity to have their say in court. Outside the courtroom, where the citizen has no way to defend himself, a prosecutor has no business speaking. That is what fairness and decency demand.

Stand by Your Man

There is one further point to make here. No official should ever be deserted by his government, or his President, in the way in which some of the victims of the Iran/Contra persecutions were deserted.

True, Congress wrote the Ethics in Government Act to leave only a glimmer of discretion for the President and his Attorney General. And true, it would take some courage for them to withstand the enormous pressure to appoint an Independent Counsel. Yet that discretion *does* exist, and the courage to exercise it ought to exist too. In the future, Presidents ought to recall the moral obligations they owe to their men, far better than did President Reagan recall the debt he owed to some of his men—men whose lives he flung into the abyss when, under heavy congressional and media pressure in 1986, he called for the appointment of an Independent Counsel in the Iran/Contra affair.

Testifying at the Gates hearing in 1991, Alan Fiers painted an illuminating, and horrifying, picture of the CIA's attitude toward its agents during that period. Gates himself, then Deputy Director, had stated with chilling clarity his view that any officer who hired a lawyer should be fired. I have noted my own amazement upon learning that the State Department's lawyers had been instructed to have nothing to do with helping me defend myself, even while I was Assistant Secretary; I was on my own. By caving in to Walsh's insistence that Department lawyers not advise Department officials whom he wished to question, the Administration was, first of all, putting a great financial burden on people not able to bear it. For most officials those burdens can be crippling. While the Ethics in Government Act provides for reimbursement of attorneys' fees for officials who have been investigated and not indicted, there is less here than meets the eye. Lawyers will tell you not to count on it. The law allows only for "reasonable" fees, which may be much lower than the fees the attorneys have actually charged. More important, the law permits reimbursement only of expenses that would not have been incurred had there been no special prosecutor, so the official may have to prove that no U.S. Attorney would ever have investigated the case. While this may be true, it will be difficult to establish. Meanwhile, retainers must be paid, and legal bills will accumulate.

But that is the least of it. The worst of it is the countenancing of such a situation altogether: permitting the whole weight of the federal government to be brought down on an official's head in an investigation that stems from his official conduct, and telling him he is on his own in defending himself. The Administration was allowing Walsh to define virtually every official witness as a possible criminal. Federal regulations allow an agency's lawyers to counsel officials until an investigation has made it clear they are at risk of prosecution. By agreeing to Walsh's demand at the outset, the Reagan Administration failed to resist the OIC's view of it as a vast criminal conspiracy just waiting to be unraveled. Officials who served their country and their President loyally deserved better.

The Reagan White House, in a panic, made a decision to cut its losses. If that meant throwing people over the side, so be it. And as those people struggled out there to stay afloat in the waves, no one was throwing them lifelines. George Shultz's defense of me was notable, and was noted, because it was such an exception. When the Administration ended, a final chance arose for the former President to come forward to defend and assist those people who had served him so well. But he remained silent, and it was a sorry performance. Presidents must demand loyalty, but they must reward it and return it as well.

AFTERWORD

January 1992

On September 16, 1991, when Craig Gillen told DeVier Pierson that there was "movement" in the investigation of me, I felt that my life had changed. By the end of 1991, I had all the proof I needed. I was no longer at risk of prosecution, but life was never going to be the same—even after the legal bills were paid.

I now had a criminal conviction, and that fact had been referred to the District of Columbia Court of Appeals for review of my status as member of the Bar. Suspension might result, or at least another round of hearings and new legal bills as I tried to prevent that suspension or, worse, disbarment. When a former client called and asked me to join him at a meeting out of town, I could not hop a plane to do so: I needed the permission of my probation officer to travel out of Washington. I needed as well to perform that hundred hours of community service, and—if it was indeed to consist of lectures on ethics issues—it would take many months to complete.

We had had some real joy hearing the things friends said to us, and satisfaction reading the editorials that praised my work and denounced the prosecution. People had written us, taken us to dinner, thrown us a party. The letters accompanying the contributions to the defense fund—many from Americans I had never met—were marvelous to read, filled with kind words and encouragement.

But there was a fact to face. This conviction was now a central feature of my life. They had pursued me for five years, almost a third of my whole working life. I had served as Assistant Secretary of State for Inter-Americans Affairs for sixteen months when the Iran/Contra scandal hit, but those sixteen months were going to overshadow all that had come before and after in my public career.

Barry Levine said to me once that we would use the phrase "ruin your life"—as in, "a criminal conviction will ruin his life"—in trying to persuade the prosecutors not to prosecute me. But don't you believe it, he told me; it won't. Don't start believing your own propaganda. Your life is your family, your friends, your work, not what Lawrence Walsh once tried to do.

He was right. This prosecution has left behind it neither sorrow nor anguish, nor any sense of defeat or of loss. It has left behind it anger. Anger that politics led a Democratic-controlled Congress to try to warp our system of justice and kept a panicky Republican White House from stopping them. Anger that officials defying that Democratic majority could be pursued as if they were criminals—indeed, pursued without even the procedural safeguards criminals are afforded in America. Anger that politics, and personal ambition, led lawyers to volunteer their services for this system of political trials.

Friends have asked me, was it worth it? Would you do it again—accept the Latin America job when Secretary Shultz offered it in the Spring of 1985, throw everything you had into a political battle that was already bitter and obviously dangerous? There were days when I wondered, days when I thought I might duck out if I had it to do over again. But those days have passed. I wish I had not been prosecuted, and I wish I had testified more carefully, but I do not wish I had refused the job. I would do it again: I would fight just as fiercely for democracy in Central America, I would speak out just as loudly in defense of a vigorous American foreign policy, I would give every ounce of my energy in the struggle we called the Cold War—and I would take the risk, which I knew was great then, that there might be a price to pay. I felt, back in 1985, that I had no other choice, and I feel that way still.

And I feel pride at how Rachel and I took their fire and survived it, survived everything the prosecutors threw at us and walked away from them smiling, with our heads high.

We are still paying that price; it is high, but not ruinous. And meanwhile, there is homework to oversee, and there are baths to give, and bedtime stories to read.

INDEX

Index